ARTHUR JAMES AND I

Also by R. W. F. Poole

HUNTING: AN INTRODUCTION

A BACKWOODMAN'S YEAR

THE RUSTIC SCRIBE

ARTHUR JAMES AND I

R. W. F. Poole

illustrations by Reg Bass

MICHAEL JOSEPH

LONDON

MICHAEL JOSEPH LTD
Published by the Penguin Group
Penguin Books Ltd, 27 Wrights Lane, London W8 5TZ, England
Viking Penguin, a division of Penguin Books USA Inc., 375 Hudson Street, New York, New York 10014, USA
Penguin Books Australia Ltd, Ringwood, Victoria, Australia
Penguin Books Canada, 10 Alcorn Avenue, Toronto, Ontario, Canada M4V 3B2
Penguin Books (NZ) Ltd, 182–190 Wairau Road, Auckland 10, New Zealand
Penguin Books Ltd, Registered Offices: Harmondsworth, Middlesex, England

First published in Great Britain 1992

Printed in England by Clays Ltd, St Ives plc
Filmset in 11½/12½ pt Monophoto Palatino

A CIP catalogue record for this book is available from the British Library
ISBN 0 7181 3437 0

I started my writing career under an alias. The reason for this was quite simple: I wanted to be able to write rude things about my friends in the morning and still be invited to drink their port wine in the evening. My father's second and third Christian names were Arthur James and this became my pen name.

The cover never really worked. For some reason people sussed out the real identity of the writer fairly quickly and if the level of dinner invitations did not fall dramatically, it was probably because not many people had ever considered inviting me in the first place. Be that as it may, Arthur James maintained.

In the early 1980s, *Shooting Times* was a very different magazine to that which appears today: it covered all Field Sports and hunting was strongly represented. Tony Jackson, the then Editor, suggested that James might contribute an occasional piece. This grew into a fortnightly column that lasted for the thick end of ten years and survived three different Editors. The column has now been consigned to the Dustbin of History, which is probably where it belongs; that, however, makes this volume of selected pieces all the more valuable.

The three Editors, Tony Jackson, Derek Bingham and Jonathan Young, all gave James a free hand, even though I have reason to believe that all of them blenched at the result on occasion. I am extremely grateful to them (and to *Shooting Times*) for their patience and forbearance. James is rather more blasé about the whole thing.

You will have noticed that I refer to James in the third person. The reason for this is that, as the column developed, and as Mr Reg Bass's brilliant drawings put the flesh on the written skeleton, James began more and more to develop a persona of his own. I regret to have to say it, but the persona was by no means an admirable one. James is greedy, lecherous (fat chance!), and noisy. He is inclined to sing when in his cups and is very inclined to be in his cups. In so far as he has political convictions, they are of the Shaggy Longhorn Tory variety. He is probably not very convinced about anything, but that does not stop him having very strong opinions and voicing them loudly on every possible (and impossible) occasion.

By now I suspect that the very thought of James makes you shudder: so what do you think it does to me? After all, I am the Frankenstein that invented this rampaging monster of the written page. There are those who are so crass as to suggest that James is in fact my alter ego, my id, my Mr Hyde. This is complete nonsense. Anyone who knows me is aware of my delicate, sensitive and retiring nature. James horrifies me, but I seem to be stuck with him. So I tiptoe gingerly through life dreading the moment when the meaty, red hand will clasp my shoulder, the hot reek of whisky and tobacco breath will wither my olfactory senses and that awful port-stained voice will bellow: 'What yer mincin' about like that for? Like some damned pinko poofter, what!?' It will be James demanding that I write another drink for him.

Mrs James is the long-suffering spouse of James. She does not figure largely because she is usually too exhausted from clearing up the trail of devastation left by James, but she does come in very handy for carrying the luggage when the Great Man goes on his travels. 'The Boy' is James's son and an appalling prospect for the future, and we must not neglect to mention Grimling. Grimling is James's butler, when he is not being dried out. He can pick a lock on a wine cellar door quicker than any man alive, but is invaluable to James because no bailiff has ever yet managed to get past him.

I have explained and apologized for James as best I can. We are indeed an odd couple, but we seem to be stuck with each other and you, the reader, must make the best of it.

Acknowledgement

These articles first appeared in *Shooting Times and Country Magazine* whom the author and publisher wish to thank for permission to reproduce them in book form.

The six chapters contain material taken from the early years of Arthur James's contributions to *Shooting Times*, and appear more or less in the order of the huntsman's year, May through to the following April.

1

It is a well known fact that all Masters of Foxhounds are warm, lovable personalities – cuddly is the word that springs to mind: they are also people of almost limitless patience. However, you will have noticed that MsFH very occasionally seem out of sorts, and there have been cases reported of Masters speaking quite sharply to members of their field, but you know how people exaggerate. You will no doubt attribute these isolated examples of humour failure to an inflamed liver or conjugal deprivation; it will never occur to you that it might be you (Yes, *you,* you idiot) what is getting right up the magisterial nose.

Let me therefore make one or two little suggestions to those who go hunting which will ease the lot of the Master, smooth his brow, and bring out that sweet little smile that makes many of the lady followers feel all warm and gooey inside.

Hounds check and your Master – who is also your huntsman – spends half an hour making highly complicated and scientific casts in the opposite direction to that taken by the hunted fox; he is looking a bit harassed as he comes down the road making plaintive noises to his bored hounds. Now is the moment to lean out of your car window, wave your half-consumed pork pie at him, and say, 'Have you lost him then?'

There is another approach to the same situation: this approach is best carried out by a mounted female follower, preferably of undeniable beauty and a low IQ. Your Master has spent the last twenty minutes going in ever decreasing circles in the same ploughed field; now let the lady follower approach (if she can contrive to trample a hound or so on her way, it will add a certain piquancy to the situation) and let her say in a beguiling way, 'Where are you going to draw next?'

All Masters are grateful for accurate information. Let us suppose that you are standing on one side of a valley and you have seen the hunted fox on the far side, a good half-mile away: hounds are also on the far side and at fault. How do you convey your information to the executive? The answer is simple: you holloa. You holloa separately and severally – you, Bill Varco, Fred Coker, Jim Pasco, old Denzil Trevithick et al. All will then be tumult and shouting: the Master, the hounds, the whole panoply of the chase will surge towards you across three badly-wired fences, a gate held together with a padlock, and that dreadful sewer of a stream in the bottom. When the whole lot arrive in a steaming pile at your feet, tell the Master that you last saw the fox a hundred yards from where he has just come, and then wait for his richly-deserved blessing. You might well wonder where Bill, Fred, Jim, and old Denzil have suddenly disappeared to.

The following is a true story: a certain Master took his hounds to a holloa; the perpetrator was standing on a roadside bank.

'Where's he gone?' asked the Master.

'I don't know but I smelled him here this morning.' Well, he *was* only trying to be helpful.

Here is another guaranteed Master tonic: you must contrive things so that your local hounds have a frustrating foxless, scentless day. On this day you must go out with the neighbouring pack, and be on your way home just in time to meet your Master boxing up his hounds prior to going home, kicking his wife and his dog, and writing out his resignation yet again. Stop, wind down your window, tell him that the Blankshire killed a leash and had a 7-mile point, and watch those craggy features break into a happy smile.

I consider all point-to-pointers to be overfed, overbred and vicious (I refer to the horses, of course), but they must be properly qualified. To achieve this happy state it is very important to bring your horse to the Master's notice. There he is sitting at the meet looking miserable. He is looking miserable because the two local shooting syndicates have decided to shoot without letting him know until the previous evening; and the Hunt Chairman has spent the last week 'laying' the only covert left (or, more accurately, pinching firewood out of it) so go and cheer him up. Ride your neurotic, rolling-eyed, toast rack right through the hounds, and ask him how long he would like you to stay out for.

All Masters like people to take an interest in and discuss their hounds, and most Masters are disappointed. There is a limit to the amount of worm balls and tail male lines that the normal hunt supporter can digest; that limit is about ninety seconds on average. This means that MsFH suffer from culture deprivation, and go about seeking people to bore; why do not you help him out.

The Hunt Ball is always a good time for chat. There he is, over in the corner of the 'night club', in a clinch with the comely and generous Mrs Bent-Fescue; you can tell it is him by the strobe-lit dandruff on his back. Go over, tap him on the shoulder and ask him what he thinks about New Forest Medyg '69.

The point of this article is to suggest that although MsFH are supermen, they are but men (unless they are women, then they are not) doing a difficult job under great pressure; they require nourishment, not punishment. I hope these little bits of advice will help people to help them.

'Be to their virtues ever kind, and to their faults a little blind.' But if you find the swine drunk in your connubial bed, please do not write and complain to me about it.

December has hardly been a happy hunting month, but surprisingly it has produced two of the best hound hunts I have been privileged to take part in. As there is not much else I can do at the moment, except the VAT return, I will tell you about them.

The first was early in the month just before all this wretched foreign weather arrived. We met up in the hill country and lots of our followers yawned and went shopping instead and serve them jolly well right.

Hounds found at once on a steep bank. Scent seemed to be

minimal but they niggled on along the bank and across to a plantation on the moor edge. There was a great roar as they fresh found and suddenly everything changed. Straight out on to the moor they went and we rammed down our hats and set off in pursuit.

It is not a nice moor to ride over, being very rocky. I was riding a new horse who had never seen a moor before. He cocked his ears, set his massive and immovable neck, and ricocheted happily from rock to rock in a rather unnerving manner.

Eventually we arrived at the top of a big dale and a grand-stand view. Hounds were several hundred feet below going down the beck, and there was the fox going steadily on through the little stone-walled fields. We could watch every twist and turn.

But not for long. Hounds were soon storming up the far side, and we had to go several hundred feet down, and then several hundred feet up to finally come up with hounds who had checked on the East Dale road. They hit it off and promptly went back down the dale, up the beck and out the other side again. Ah well. It was fortunate that the scent was holding rather than screaming.

We eventually got to them doing some very pretty work through several fields of Swaledale sheep. The horses got a well-earned breather, then again on and off the moor, and down into a great wooded dale that is, as they say, lifting with foxes. Our fox ran the forestry tracks here, but the hounds never faltered and pushed him right through and out the other side.

As hounds came out of the top of the covert, they seemed to surge forward and suddenly our tired horses were having to really gallop to keep in any sort of touch. The fox circled back to the covert and dropped down to the river. The cry changed. He crossed the river but could not make it up the far dale side and turned back into a beech plantation where the end came. By his teeth, he was a first season cub but he had stood up in front of hounds for 22 miles and 2¾ hours. Just a fair hunt.

Next day the iron frosts came and then the snow. Conditions have been so bad that the horses cannot even get up the lane from the stables.

Boxing Day found us in freezing fog and 4 inches of snow, shivering in the Market Square waiting to hunt on our feet, with a surprisingly large crowd of people assembled.

It has been said of our Master huntsman that he is no horseman. He is no Sebastian Coe either, being built on the lines of a badly-designed brick khazi. By the bye, he is strong favourite to win the Dangler Trophy. This is a challenge trophy presented annually at Harrogate Hound Show, to the Master kennelled north of the Trent who has made the largest live weight gain in the last twelve months. His main rival (York and Ainsty South) is rumoured to be suffering from nervous dyspepsia, so get your money on now.

Anyway, there was our Master looking like a pillar box with tackety boots, and off we all slid, stumbled and shuffled and fairly quickly found a fox. I think what followed was a really rather amazing day. There was a crust of the snow that carried the fox but not the hounds, and they must have put in some extraordinary hard work. The surprising thing was that there was a scent.

One hears a lot of criticism of the cars and Land-Rovers spoiling sport, but that day was theirs. There were no nasty horses to get in their way and without them we should never have kept in touch.

Hounds kept going in an inexorable fashion; frozen rivers, roads, icy tracks, they could hunt them all. It was a strange scent that seemed to be exactly the same whether the fox was one minute or twenty in front. No holloa or distraction could make them lift their heads; it was lovely hound work. The Master paraphrased Sir Henry Bentinck and said, 'They hunt so well when I'm not there to —— it up for them.'

There was some desperate thrusting and some vivid pictures remain.

The peaceful inhabitants of a market town staring in amazement at a dozen Land-Rovers in close column and at maximum revs, with people hanging on in every possible, and impossible, position.

The Land-Rover setting off very suddenly with its unwary riders dropping off the back like ripe fruit.

A Lady Master being hauled into the back of an accelerating Land-Rover by an arm and a leg.

A moving cloud of steam said to contain our Master; anyway we think it was because someone handed in a whisky bottle and it came out again half empty.

We did not catch the fox, but hounds were eventually stopped in the dark having run 20 miles and having made a 5-mile point.

It was a Boxing Day to remember.

I was talking to the Duke of X the other day. It is one of the great regrets of my life that I was not born to be a duke; I think it would be such fun. X obviously did not think it was fun, and would have been much happier working in Woolworths. I wonder if we could do a swap? I am frankly getting desperate, the chances of my getting en-dukled legally seem to be receding and unless I get there soon I shall be too old to enjoy all the fun of breeding my own estate workers.

I shall just have to keep practising quietly and hope that my elevation is not too far off.

How I hate snow. I am pretty weatherproof on the whole, and can shrug my shoulder and get on with it in most conditions, but snow is different. We have had snow in excessive quantities, in my opinion. There is no question of hunting. A nice lady asked me if we could not take hounds to the forestry on foot. I asked her if she had been out that way lately: she said that she had not. I did not think she had as the forestry is twenty miles away, well hidden behind twenty-foot snowdrifts. Anyway I thanked her politely for the suggestion.

I was discussing the weather with a retired shepherd and he told me something that I had never heard before: for good weather the wind needs to change clockwise, as it might be from south to west. If it goes the other way, say east to north, then look out. It seems to make sense.

It is often the case that a lay-off is preceded by a particularly good day. Scenting conditions are at their best just before cold weather comes. I have been poking through my hunting diaries. I always find it a bother to keep them up, but they are great fun to look back through. My diary accounts are pretty terse but evoke many memories, some fond and some sour, but mostly good. But enough of these mawkish reminiscences. The point is that the diaries show that what I consider to have have been the three great hunts that I have taken part in were all followed by spells of bad weather. Two of these hunts were 10-mile points, one on Dartmoor and one in Yorkshire. Both ended in the dark without catching the fox and were therefore slightly unsatisfactory. I do recall, however, both resulted in the consumption of large quantities of whisky.

The finest hound hunt I have yet had happened in Yorkshire. It was a brilliant clear frosty day. Hounds found at 11.20 and killed a huge dog fox at 3.50. In that time, they ran 25 miles in two large circles and were only touched once, when a slight adjustment was necessary due to some over-enthusiastic car followers. I shall never forget listening to hounds below me in a big wooded dale just before the end; they had the fox beat and they knew it. I do not think I have ever heard quite such a cry; it really did make my back hairs stand up.

Back to being snowbound. An MFH in these conditions is not a lovesome thing, God wot. I sat around the fire with Mrs James the other evening while the blizzard screamed outside, and we compiled lists of MsFH with whom we would like to be snowed up. Our lists were not similar in all respects, which is just as well. I might publish the lists (suitably annotated) when I am old enough not to care whether I get asked out to dinner again. But when you really boil it down, the fact is that if you are going to be snowed up with somebody, choose very carefully, and if I were you I should on no account choose an MFH.

There is a sad little story. A certain Border MFH, maddened by the sight of ever-increasing Caledonian snowdrifts, packed the magisterial carpetbag and fled to Exmoor in frustrated fury and a motor car. This MFH then found himself in the happy position of being able to compare the size, density and general condition of Exmoor snowdrifts with their Scottish equivalent.

For those of us who cannot take flight for more temperate climes, there are lots of merry ploys to keep us amused, mainly concerned with getting things into drifts and then digging them out: it is all great fun and the healthy exercise thus engendered helps to remove the evil humours that might otherwise brew up within the breast. A 20-mile round trip for some hay took me six hours, and I considered myself fortunate to get there and back at all.

My problems are as nothing to those being suffered by people up in the hills, many of whom are completely cut off and have been for the thick end of a week. Last summer I bought a Daihatsu 4X4. I had been pleased with it up until now; it makes nothing of towing two horses, or forty fat lambs. But it has been really impressive in the snow; I should have been in severe trouble without it.

I tried to telephone a friend of mine in the fells to see how he was faring, but his telephone was deep frozen. I do not suppose that I should have heard anything to cheer me up. There is, however, a certain cold comfort in everybody being in the same boat.

What is really tiresome is to be having a bad run of sport for whatever reason, and to be rung up by someone you have always considered to be a friend, and to have to listen to a yard by yard account of 'the run of the century'. You sit there, knuckles whitening as you try to strangle the telephone, with the sour bile of jealousy rising in your throttle. As the joyous baying at the other end subsides, you manage to force some form of congratulation through gritted teeth, and slam the receiver down before he can ask you what sort of sport you are having – he knows before he telephoned, anyway. Of course, your reaction is very childish, the nice man was only trying to cheer you up; that is what friends are for.

It will be a bad day if telephones ever get fitted with viewing screens. You would no longer be able to say, with great sincerity, 'I'd love to talk but I'm literally just dashing out of the door', if the caller can see you with your slippers on and your pipe firing on all cylinders. We would all have to be truthful and sincere, like my feed merchant when I rang him the other day, who opened with: 'Have you paid your bill yet?' On balance, I am all for a little insincerity; it helps make the world go round.

I find it very difficult to write about hunting flasks as I never carry one; but I do expect all members of my field to carry them and to lose no opportunity of offering them to me. This probably explains why I attract ever-dwindling fields.

I offer two recipes from opposite ends of the country: the first is the Percy Special which is reputed to have been invented by His Grace of Northumberland. It consists of equal parts whisky and cherry brandy and is just the thing when the Siberian wind comes sweeping over Alnwick. One cautionary note: this drink has a time fuse and does not really grip for about half an hour, when paralysis sets in.

Mazawattee Tea is Cornish and full of Celtic perfidy. It is gin and cider in various proportions. It also has delayed action and has the added refinement of attacking the legs first. This means that you can carry on a highly intelligent and stimulating conversation whilst scratching your left ear with your right foot.

2

I can honestly say that throughout my hunting career I have never jumped a fence. I have been carried over them by good horses. I have been buried in them by bad horses. As a scientific equitator my rating is zero. This makes me an ideal person to write an informed article on horses and fences, rather like the well-known journalist who wrote heartrending and much praised articles on Bangladesh from a hotel penthouse in Calcutta.

The 'Yellow' Earl of Lonsdale was a famous horseman. I understand that one of his party pieces was to position two dinner plates on the take-off side of a fence and two on the landing: he would then place his horse so exactly as to break all four. I have broken a lot of plates in my time, but never by skilled horsemanship.

My equitation consists of pointing my horse at the obstacle, grabbing a fistful of mane, closing my eyes and saying a brief but sincere prayer.

When my smart friends are banging on about 'collecting' their horses and 'stride', I just say in a superior manner, 'I never interfere with my horse when jumping.'

I was brought up in a bank country and I suppose banks are the obstacles that frighten me least. Banks are approached at a sensible pace and if, having gained the summit, you find the prospect less than pleasing, as it might be a man with a double-breasted gun, you can turn round and return whence you came.

I came by my best banking horse by accident. I was out hunting on a new horse that did not want to start; a farmer friend was out on a new horse that did not want to stop. We changed horses and saddles in the middle of a field. We both had a good day and went home with each other's horses.

Would that all problems of mounting could be so easily solved.

In an open hill country, blood is of prime importance. Common horses cannot go up hill, and having eventually reached the top are unlikely to take you down the other side either quickly or safely. In bogs, they will panic and plunge then sink and sulk. A good moor horse skitters through the 'stuggy' taking small quick steps.

I had a marvellous moor horse who was polo pony bred. He would not jump a pole lying on the ground, but what a hill horse. He was the fastest downhill horse I have ever ridden. It was quite impossible to steady him at all; he had six legs and was as quick and as sure as a cat. He never put a foot wrong and used to bounce from rock to rock. He did wonders for my grip.

Some years later I was trying to hunt hounds in a stiffish vale country with a hard riding field and I lost my nerve. My wife solved the problem by appointing Uncle Stanley as my hunting nanny. Uncle Stanley was a little whippet of a man with a permanent grin from ear to ear whose great love was jumping fences. His two great cries were: 'Come on, Master, let's have this bugger,' as we approached a blackthorn Maginot line, and 'Bugger, us made the wire ping there,' as we landed more or less on the other side. I never see a nasty wirey fence without a fond memory of Uncle Stanley.

Except on my annual bath night I normally avoid water. Open water is probably an unusual obstacle in most hunting countries today. However, there are parts of the West Country where the fields are separated by large dykes or rhynes (pronounced reens). These obstacles have the great advantage from a Master's point of view, of being completely unbreakable no matter how many horses have jumped them. A rhyne consists of 18 inches or so depth of stagnant water over primeval ooze apparently without bottom. If you get your horse in one, people will fetch a tractor and ropes to extract it. If you fall in one, they won't.

I had a horse who fell in a rhyne with me and then sat on me and sulked; with great presence of mind I managed to get my horn out and used it as a snorkel until help arrived.

On another occasion, my horse took off, suddenly realized it was over water, stopped in mid air, hovered for an eternity, and then dropped like a stone into the gunge.

The best way to take water on a horse is well diluted with whisky.

The Grockle season is drawing to a close. I am fortunate enough to live and work in a very beautiful part of England but from April to the end of September we are infested with Grockles.

Grockles are holiday makers and I do not know how the word originated; the Cornish call them 'Emmetts' (Cornish for ant) which somehow sounds less rude. But I fear both words are denigrative, and the feeling behind them is selfish but human. I have two blocks of land, five miles apart, and I fully admit that I regard the lanes in between them as my private road. I get cross when I am in a hurry and find the roads blocked with caravans, flocks of bicyclists, and straggling columns of juvenile hikers all of whom make obscene gestures at me as I creep through their ranks in bottom gear.

Please do not think that I am against people enjoying the beauties of the country, I am only against the inconvenience they cause *me*.

My sheep-handling pens are hard beside a road leading to a famous beauty spot. When I am 'fettling sheep' – which covers all the myriad ovine tasks – in the summer, I can guarantee a line of camera-clicking onlookers down the roadside fence and I do not mind this at all. They are invariably nice people and a bit of crack with them relieves the monotony that soiled sheeps' backsides can induce. Photographs of my rear end must be the high spot of many a family album.

I do not mind them picnicking in my fields, but I do mind when they leave the gate open afterwards and let all my sheep out. This is inconvenient.

It is all selfish and rather irrational. When I am rushing back to get whatever item of equipment I have inevitably forgotten, and I come hard up behind the car containing the family party admiring the countryside at 15mph (always with the windows tight shut), I get cross. Do they not know what a hurry I am in?

It is quite a different story when the old David Brown is chugging back over the hill at 3mph with a load of hay behind, filling the lane from side to side. I puff my pipe and chuckle. I cannot see them but they will be there, a growing line of sweating humanity, big cars, small cars, caravans – and no passing place for at least a mile.

Let them wait, it is quite intolerable all this rushing about.

People are in far too much of a hurry these days; are they not on holiday anyway?

I was judging In-Hand Combine Harvesters at the Blankshire Show (I am the definitive expert in this difficult art) when I met an eminent MFH. After I had tugged my forelock, I asked when he hoped to start hunting.

'As late as I possibly can, old boy,' he said. Well really, what a thing to say.

I love the autumn hunting. To me the first morning comes as fresh and exciting every year as it did – well, quite a long time ago anyway. When it does not, I shall know it is time to give up hunting hounds.

By the end of August, the summer has gone stale, and hound exercise has become a definite pain in the base area. I know that there are people who claim to love hound exercise, but on closer investigation you usually find that they only go twice a year themselves.

But there comes a time when there is a sharpness in the evening air, when the mists lie heavy in the morning, and when the trees start to turn from their tired cabbagey green; there is that special tang of autumn in the air; hunting cannot be far away.

Autumn is a special time for Masters and huntsmen. It is their private time when they need think of nothing but their hounds. It is a time of education for young hounds and young foxes and must be respected as such. In recent years, there has been a tendency for hunt committees to nibble away at the cubhunting season by capping people in October. This is wrong. Even six weeks is little enough time to get young hounds settled into their work. If you are going to allow them only a fortnight and, in some seasons, only a week before the ladies and gentlemen start playing football with them, then you are giving them very little chance indeed.

Some countries are more fortunate than others when it

comes to getting an early start, but the vast majority of hunts cannot start until the bulk of the corn is cut; do not start until you have room for four clear mornings, I was always told.

Arable Masters get very twitchy towards the end of harvest, and spend a lot of time on the telephone, biting their finger nails, and driving about with a pair of binoculars and a nervous tic.

I suppose the second week in September would be about the average start time for most hunts these days. Looking back through my diaries I find that the latest I have ever started was 16 September and the earliest 23 August. Of course, there are those fortunate countries who can start when they like. I know a woodland Master who often starts in July, and several hill and moorland Masters who start in August. They have, too, the great advantage of being able to set a firm starting date, regardless of conditions. This is a great help in planning hound exercise. I suppose most of us have miscalculated at some time, and got our hounds too fit too early and been caught by the weather; the resultant delay can be very hairy indeed.

Another advantage of starting early is that you can get round the country properly and have time to sort out the big strongholds.

There has been an increase in evening cubhunting during the last few years, and this has apparently proved very popular. It does have the advantage that the scent is likely to improve as the night comes on. I am afraid that I have never really taken to the idea: for me, there is no substitute for the feel and smell of the early morning.

I suppose the answer is to do what a friend of my father's used to do: start off in the morning with one pack, knock off at lunchtime and send the hounds home; then the hamper would be brought up and a tidy bit of luncheon taken on charge followed by a pipe and forty winks. By this time the other pack had been brought out and the afternoon shift could begin.

How long is a morning's cubhunting? About as long as the proverbial piece of string. I normally reckon four to five hours is probably enough, but so much depends on the circumstances. The shortest morning I ever had was half an hour. We went to a thorn covert where there was a strong breed of cubs. This covert had a peculiarity: some twenty years before it had been laid and as the covert grew up this layer had grown up with it, forming a sort of penthouse suite at the top of the thorns.

Hounds were put in and found at once. They ran with a tremendous cry for half an hour by which time every fox in the covert had taken the lift to the top floor and there was absolutely nothing we could do. Since there was nowhere else available to hunt, we went home.

The longest morning I ever had was when we left kennels at 0915 and got back at 2345; suffice it to say that at about 1500 we had marked in 'only a rabbits' bury; about ten minutes'.

There is often argument as to the best sort of place to start hunting – big woods, small woods, hedgerows: in fact, you generally start where you can and make the best of it. The one thing you must make certain about in advance is that there is likely to be a litter of cubs when you get there; a blank first morning is pretty demoralizing all round.

As to the conduct of Autumn hunting; to hold up or not to hold up, that will depend on individual circumstances and country. But let it be conducted *quietly*; let the young hounds learn from the *cry* of their elders and have nothing else to distract them.

One of the most shocking mornings of my life was spent cubhunting with a very famous pack, and the noise was unbelievable; if the massed bands of the Foot Guards had been in the covert I do not think they would have been noticed.

I can hardly wait for the moment when that little whimper in the bracken signals the finding of the first fox of another season.

A little clash of cultures story. A couple bought a largish house in a certain hunting country. I think they designed PVC knickers for pop stars or something similarly esoteric, and the husband liked shooting things. They were very friendly and keen for the local hunt to meet at their house. With this in mind, the Master rang them up during the season and spoke to the housekeeper.

No, Mr and Mrs X were not in.

Well, he was ringing up to fix for the hounds to meet at the house.

Oh there was no need for that now. Mr X shot the fox last

week. They had it in the deep freeze, and Mr X had taken it up to London in a plastic bag yesterday.

So if you go shopping fashionably, look out for a PVC jockstrap with fox-fur lining.

It is as predictable as influenza in the typing pool. Every year in the sporting press, there is a rash of letters on the inflammatory subject of Hunting and the Top Hat.

The letters are entirely predictable and are divided between those who wear top hats and are struggling to get out of them; and those who view their struggle complacently from beneath the brim of a hunting cap. There will also be a letter from the inimitable Bertie Luce-Rayne (Maj) saying that he has fallen through his top hat with twenty-three different packs of hounds, and it has never done him any harm, and what is more he is damned proud to wear a top hat. He can't think what all these damned fellers are whining about etc., etc.

I have never worn a top hat except on a single occasion when I was press-ganged into a hunt team at the Devon County Show. Both events are strictly non-recurring as far as I am concerned. However, I do thoroughly sympathize with the

Mad Hatters. Like sex, the top hat looks ridiculous and is damnably expensive, but I doubt if it affords its wearer the slightest titillation.

From a practical point of view, if you fall on your top hat, you will certainly bend the hat and most likely yourself as well. As a piece of protective head gear, the top hat rates zero.

The only sensible headpiece for hunting is a hunting cap, properly made and properly fitted so that it stays on the head without benefit of elastic 'neath the chin. Nor do we want those extraordinary tangles of webbing straps. However, on reflection, I can see some good in them if they are buckled so tight as to preclude the wearer opening its mouth.

Now we come to the tricky bit. You have honourably retired your top hat and are using it as a pending tray for the pile of buff envelopes marked OHMS.

You have bought your cap.

What are you going to wear with it apart from a Damart vest, and drawers, cotton, cellular, pairs, one?

'My red coat, of course,' you will say. 'Not so,' say the Masters. 'Red coats and hunting caps must remain the privilege of hunt staff and officials; can't have just any Tom, Dick and Harry swanning about in 'em.'

'Oh very well, if you're going to be so stuffy I'll wear a black coat with a hunting cap,' you say rather huffily.

'For shame, for shame (or some such),' say the farmers, 'that is *our* uniform and indicates that we have the privilege of galloping straight across our neighbours' wheat. Can't have just any fool dressed like that.'

So you are once more reduced to your Damart vest and drawers, cellular, and to seeking a solution.

Some years ago I did an American tour, which is another story, but in its course I attended a point-to-point 'somewhere in Virginia'. I remember being fascinated by the 'Hon Whip' who was stationed in front of me; his breeches had obviously been made by Hitler's tailor; his coat had been built to allow for future development on the existing site; he was wearing shades (sun glasses to you) and chewing gum – but all that was as nothing to his cap. His cap was bright emerald green.

I found this fantastic vision much more interesting than the point-to-point. After all, as a recent Vice President of the US of A might have said, 'When you have seen one point-to-point, you have seen them all.'

The scar left by the memory of the green cap has stayed with me over the years, and was reopened the other day. One of our subscribers produced a guest from the Celtic mists of the west and, my dear, he came wearing a red coat and a *grey* hunting cap! It was too, too riveting; one almost expected lots of large policemen to thunder up and start wrapping their tunics round him. I think our old-fashioned foxes were appalled by the sight because we had a blank day. However, it transpired that the guest's Master had sanctioned the wearing of grey caps as an alternative to top hats. It certainly looks better than emerald green but just not quite kosher.

So now we have got our followers kitted out in properly fitted caps of a sober hue; what next?

Next should come a properly tied stock tie in which art the Pony Club should run courses, and this will bring us to the coat and the point where readers of a choleric or liverish disposition are advised to inhale deeply.

We have already agreed that reprieve from a top hat does not necessarily entitle a person to wear a red or black coat with his hunting cap. So he must have a different coloured coat. How simply is the problem solved by the use of a little native wit.

The vexed question is what is to be the colour of this new coat? This requires some thought. I do not recommend yellow; it looks well enough on the Berkeley staff but I should think it is hell's delight to clean.

A dark blue coat would be a good sensible colour but that has become the uniform of a very eminent personage.

A good dark, bottle green would be a practical hard-wearing colour, and should not show the stains too much if you are in the habit of dribbling port at the meet, or wallowing in a peat hag.

But I think the colour I favour most is grey. An eminent soldier used to hunt with me on occasion and he always wore a coat of Hodden Grey and uncommon smart he looked too. I understand that this was the kind of coat that John Peel wore and if it was good enough for him, it will certainly be good enough for any of you.

I suppose you will all insist on wearing those awful white nylon breeches. If you must, then please wear white garter straps and remember that it is not enough to clean them once a year. And please keep your Clan Cameron tartan socks inside your boots, not with half a yard flowing out over the tops.

I think we have resolved that problem very neatly, but if you reject my ideas and insist on your red coat, then the only answer is another form of head gear.

There is a charming item of military equipment called: 'Pots, Chamber, Rubber, Officers Lunatic for the use of'. Somewhere there is almost certainly an ordnance store over-flowing with these useful articles far exceeding the supply of 'Officers, Lunatic' (I hope). If these were sold off by the War Office they could provide a practical, and distinctive, answer to the Hunting Head Gear problem.

After all, we must not get too po-faced about these things.

The other day we drew a covert blank. It was a vulpine haven that used to hold so many foxes that people groaned when they heard that they were going there. Now it is foxless; the pheasants have destroyed them utterly, and yet the owner of these vulpicidal pheasants is a hunting man.

What I dislike is the man who claims to support hunting, who tells you that there will always be foxes on his land but you know and he knows that his particular keeper is intent on murdering every fox he can, safe in the knowledge that his employer will never say boo to him: the employer is frightened of the employee.

Over a hundred years ago Surtees remarked on how strange it was that people employed servants to rule over them: he was talking about a huntsman, and indeed this is a situation not unknown today. It has been known to happen with butlers and farm managers, but it is very common with gamekeepers. I remember a certain estate that was completely terrorized by the old headkeeper who demanded and got the dismissal of any estate employee who crossed him.

I suppose you could argue, well, good luck to the keeper: but I do not believe that the tail wagging the dog is a proper proceeding.

I have met peers of the realm, steely-eyed captains of industry, ancient and valiant soldiers, men who would strip an asset naked, without a qualm, or rob a machine gun nest, yet rather than face the disapproval of their keeper they will hide, whimpering, in the estate office. It is passing strange.

Would that they were all like the landowner who was asked by a new keeper what should be done about foxes and who replied tersely, 'No foxes; no keeper'; an admirable maxim.

It has been said (with justice) that all ex MsFH are vermin. I am an ex MFH several times over, but I have always had the good sense to leave the ex-country as quickly as possible and certainly before the bailiff's men arrive.

All ex MsFH regard their successors with suspicion, at best. They are convinced that the new man will ruin the hounds, the country and, worst of all, all the nubile females who have found the Ex too old and smelly and who welcome a bit of fresh flesh.

For the first time, I am still living in a country that I recently relinquished, and were it not for the happy fact that my time is fully occupied elsewhere, I know that I should be just as big a pain in the rear echelons as my predecessors. It is most comforting to find that I am human, if verminous, after all.

One of the problems caused by reaching the peak of one's profession (and how else can a contributor to *Shooting Times* be regarded) is that one is always being importuned by more or less worthy causes for support and sponsorship. Most of these appeals I can reject with a clear conscience: I have no wish to support Gay Liberation in the Vale of Evesham, nor do I intend to join the platform party at a rally to Save the Brown Rat. However, every now and then something breaks through my adamantine defences. I am not ashamed to say that after reading the appeal from SAMBO I was forced to get out my BFSS red-spotted handkerchief and have a jolly good blow. What is SAMBO? Well I think the best thing I can do is to reproduce the letter from Lady Feele-Boote who is patroness of the Society.

> SAM stands for Save Ancient Masters and I am afraid the BO speaks for itself.
>
> Have you ever wondered about what happens to old Masters of Foxhounds? To most of you, an MFH is an imposing figure, a symphony in scarlet, black and white mounted on a shining blood horse: the very epitome of virility and manly virtue, in the prime of life.
>
> But you know he will not always be like that. The years will take their toll. Eyes will become less bright, limbs less supple. The wear and tear of hard days and nights spent in the service of foxhunting will leave

their ineradicable mark on body and temper; and the bank will foreclose.

What is to become of these unhappy creatures once they have received their farewell pat from the Hunt Chairman and their statutory presentation Ingersoll pocket watch? Is there no alternative to a call from the plain van from the MFHA and a despatch to that great Chairman in the sky?

This is where SAMBO comes in. Our organization aims to find kind twilight homes for these pathetic old creatures where they can live out their last days in peace and reasonable sobriety.

Taking in an old Master is not easy and requires a very special sort of person. It has to be said that they are usually smelly and their personal habits leave a lot to be desired, but the organization does supply, free of charge, a special heavy duty mortice lock for fitting on your wine cellar.

The difficulties are many but so are the compensations. When your Master lays his great purple jowled face on your knee, and looks up at you lovingly with those tiny bloodshot eyes, or when he curls up contentedly at the foot of your bed, then you will experience that very special sensation that comes as the result of a very special act of kindness (you will find paracetamol a great help).

So if you think you could provide comfort and security for one of these verminous old morons, just write to or ring SAMBO and our hound van will call on you with a selection for you to choose from.

Thank you all so much.

The *Shooting Times* is always at the sharp end of new developments in hunting. I am proud to announce a further step forward and report that a new challenge cup will be competed for at a major hound show this summer. This is the

Shooting Times Challenge Trophy (a tasteful EPNS model of the Spirit of Unbridled Lubricity) and is a trophy with a difference: it is a competition for Masters, not for hounds.

It must be stated at once that this class will be confined to Male Masters; there will be no Bi——, I mean Lady class. No discrimination is intended; it is just that the sponsors have rightly concluded that no one is going to be brave, or stupid, enough to judge a class of Lady Masters.

The class will be judged in the usual way on looks, conformation and movement. Let me give you some idea of what the judges will be looking for:

Looks: it is important that an MFH should look like an MFH; long hair and limp wrists will be definitely out. A good purple face is obviously a plus point, but bloodshot eyes and bottle noses will be penalized on the grounds of expense, temper and potential unsoundness.

A dark suit that fits, and well-polished black shoes with toecaps will create a good impression, but do not let your entry polish his toecaps on the backs of his trousers in the ring.

The stiff collar should be tight enough to allow the neck to bulge over it. The Master should be made to wash at least down as far as his collar.

Conformation: There are two main types of Master: the old-fashioned rather heavy type with dewlaps and bristling moustaches, usually found floundering about in bottomless plough countries. This type is now rather being superseded by the 'Super Ferret' type that tends to go wizardly fast across country, through marriages, and out of pocket.

Of course, the type favoured will depend on the judges and many a stimulating ringside argument will result.

Movement: This was thought to present quite a problem, as it is obviously a waste of time expecting MsFH to chase bits of biscuit. The problem has been solved neatly by the technical department. An electrified rail will be run around the showring with a little trolley on which will be a silver salver with a glass and a decanter of port. With this in motion, the following stampede will enable the judges to spot any faults in movement.

It was suggested that some contestants might take a short cut across the ring, but to do this they would require human intelligence: if they had that, they would hardly be Masters of Hounds, would they?

(Stop Press: Evens the W. Percy.)

A lady telephoned me the other day in a high state of excitement to say that having long since lost her nerve out hunting, she had now restored it. What a strange thing nerve is: Somerville and Ross put it very succintly: 'It is my belief that six out of every dozen people who go out hunting are disagreeably conscious of a nervous system, and two out of the six are in what is brutally called "a blue funk."'

Unlike the lady above, whom I heartily congratulate, I have never had any nerve and I have always gone hunting in a blue funk. When I was younger, I was what an eminent horseman called a 'hard funk', and worked on the principle that if I closed my eyes and went fast enough at an obstacle I was likely to get to the other side. As a method of crossing a country, this idea leaves a lot to be desired and the progressive failure rate will produce a corresponding increase in the blueness of your funk.

When I remarked to someone the other day that I had 'lost my bottle', he wondered what bottle had to do with nerve, apart from the obvious correlation. I did not know; it is simply one of those demotic phrases that one acquires if one spends much time in the earthier levels of society.

However, now I do know: bottle and glass are rhyming slang for, well, for backside, and two hundred years ago a person with nerve was said to have 'bottom'.

Digging in the same rich vein, I also discovered the derivation of 'Berk' which has to do with foxhunting and anatomy: think about it, and while you are doing so, I am going to potter off to the pub to replenish my 'bottle'.

I love quotations. I have the sort of mind that is quite incapable of absorbing information of a practical nature, but is a positive bonded warehouse of arcane and useless trivia.

I can quote just enough Shakespearian and Latin tags to be accused of scholarly leanings by foxhunters; equally, I know just enough about hunting to pass as a venator amongst scholars. Where I really cut an arser is where I meet a scholarly foxhunter who can paste my pretensions with both barrels, leaving only the beak and claws to mark their passing.

However, we are not going to concern ourselves with culture: 'de minimis Lex non curat' as the solicitor said when he refused the pudding – 'the Law does not concern itself with trifles'; geddit? We are going to consider some useful little hunting aphorisms.

Many years ago when I was brewing up for my first mastership, I was talking to a very senior huntsman and he gave me one of the best bits of advice anyone could give an embryonic MFH: 'If you try to please everybody, you will end by pleasing nobody. Try to please yourself and with a bit of luck you will please one or two others as well.' I thoroughly recommend this maxim; it has saved me from the odd nervous collapse.

Another piece of excellent advice is, 'Always park your troubles outside the Kennels.' Hounds will only give 100% for you if you give 100% for them. They sense what sort of mood you are in at once: if you are going to spend your hunting day thinking of all the things you would have said to your wife, if only you had thought of them in time, then do not expect much of the day's hunting.

I once hunted a particularly difficult and tiresome country and was helped through it by my kennel huntsman who not only taught me a lot, but was, and is, one of the funniest men I know.

Once we were having a bad patch; my morale was rock bottom and this was showing itself in the hounds. I asked his advice: 'Winners never quit, and quitters never win,' he said and how right he is. I pulled myself together and *tried*, and things improved. I still use that quotation to make myself try that bit harder and it is sometimes that bit that saves a hunting day.

This same man (this is going to cost me a fortune next time I see him) was full of handy sayings. I suppose one of the fascinations about hunting hounds is that it is a difficult thing to do well, or as X (let us call him) used to say: 'If hunting hounds was easy, my missus could do it; and if my missus could do it, any silly b—— could do it.' I must add that this was a gross slander on his charming wife.

Another salutary little thought is that 'a huntsman is only as good as his last day's hunting': in other words, no huntsman can rest on any laurels he may have managed to gather.

No reputation is so hardly won, nor so easily lost as that of a huntsman.

I once took a knowledgeable friend of mine autumn hunting with the Blankshire: there were lots of foxes and lots of hounds, but neither seemed disposed to exert themselves unduly. I asked my friend how he had enjoyed his morning. 'Like watching paint dry,' was his laconic reply.

3

There is a shortage of Masters of Fox Hounds or, to be more precise, of *trained* Masters of Fox Hounds. We live in a complex age and if foxhunting is to come through unscathed it is going to need knowledgeable, professional leadership. No one who has had experience in foxhunting over the last twenty years can doubt the vastly increased professionalism of the MFHA for which we should all give bounteous thanks. But if GHQ is sound, what then is the state of the regimental officers? That, my dears, is the warp and weave of the matter.

There are some very able Masters today, and a few brilliant practitioners in the field and out of it. There are also some moderate Masters, and some are very moderate indeed.

I suggest that Foxhunting is a profession, and a highly skilled and demanding one at that. It is also a wolf pit. Into this pit every season is thrown an annual offering of persons young and not so young; their only protection the title Master of Fox Hounds and, if they are literate, a copy of Beckford. Some win through, but the bones of the failures are many and well chewed.

Let me give you an example.

Once upon a time there was a young man who had a great love of foxhunting, in fact it was about his only asset. At the ripe age of twenty-three he applied for a Mastership, and rather to everyone's surprise he was accepted and entered upon his duties on the 1st of May, pink and shining with enthusiasm. From 2 May onwards he was an unmitigated disaster. His kennel huntsman regarded him in the same light as an attack of piles. His hounds sneered at him openly. Socially he was regarded as a jest in doubtful taste, and the local damselry whom he had fondly imagined pounding on his door in fevered droves, fled from him as fast as they were able to with crossed thighs.

When he paraded at the local show, his hounds all went to the fun fair leaving him alone in the ring wailing sadly on his horn.

The Puppy Show was a shambles.

By the end of autumn hunting, the foxes voted him Huntsman of the Year.

He sent in his resignation the night of the Opening Meet. The next morning two senior and formidable ladies of the hunt appeared in the yard; one soundly boxed his ears, the other bit him in the calf. They gave him to understand that from now on he would do as they told him, not for his own miserable sake but for the sake of foxhunting.

He did, and thanks to the Senior and Formidable Ladies he survived. Seventeen seasons on he is still surviving and is still mindful of the debt of gratitude he owes to the S and F Ladies.

Not everyone is so lucky. Every year keen young men, and women, come on the scene, bursting with enthusiasm and ignorance, and fail. This is wasteful, unnecessary and bad for foxhunting all round. There is a lot at stake. Nothing succeeds like success. A well-run hunt should be something with which local people are proud to identify whether they hunt actively or not. The future of hunting as a whole depends on this grass roots support. No hunt is so small or unimportant that it can be allowed to become a shambles that no one wants to identify with. A well-run hunt will produce stable employment for good men and will do its bit to maintaining and improving that most splendid of animals, the foxhound.

The fish stinks from the head; you cannot have a well-run hunt without proper direction and this means *trained* Masters. But how to achieve this desirable end?

I have a vision of some form of National Foxhunting College where young hopefuls would be sent to read for a degree in Vulpine Sciences. I might even consider the post of Master provided that I got an honorary D.Vulp and free range of the generously endowed cellar.

Sound principles of management in Kennel and Field would be taught, but the College would basically be run on the 'Sickener' principle, invented for SAS recruits. The shooting would be let to a syndicate of carefully selected Birmingham business magnates, and tended by a particularly malignant covey of keepers from Kirkcudbrightshire.

There would be two Home Farms: one would be run by a man from deepest Norfolk dedicated to winter corn and the total eradication of every possible tree and hedge. The other farm would be run by two spinster ladies who kept goats and Jersey cows.

Particular emphasis would be put on teaching students to resist the three Ls that have been the downfall of so many Masters: Language, Liquor and Lust. To combat these evils there would be regular busloads of members of Whites, whose fathers had all been Masters of the Whaddon Chase for one season. On the strength of this, they would pontificate separately and severally on exactly how hunting should be conducted.

There would be the 'Farm Run' where students would have to visit ten 'farms' in five hours, at each of which they would be plied with whisky, Bristol Cream, Percy Specials and cider; they would then take tea with the Resident Dowager Duchess.

Last, but not least, there would be the entrancing lady whose 'boring old husband spent all week in the City leaving her all on her little own'. (Different arrangements would be made for female students.)

However, in this less than perfect world I fear that this vision will remain just that, but I do not think it too fanciful to suggest that anyone desirous of taking on hounds should first spend a period apprenticed to an established MFH. Masters have to be made like any other young animal and what better way to learn than by good example and advice, and a thick ear when necessary.

It would be time well spent. The embryonic Master would learn to avoid many snares and delusions. The training time would also give the aspirant, and others, a chance to find out whether indeed he was suited to set out on the cold, hard road of Mastership. Better a small private disappointment than the trauma that a later public failure would inflict not only on him but on a whole hunting country.

As to the type of person likely to become a Master of Fox Hounds, the great Lord Willoughby de Broke wrote: 'No one is too good to be a Master of Fox Hounds. If he be gifted with the average endowment of tact, administrative talent, power of penetrating character, and all other attributes that form the essential equipment of a successful public man, so much the better.'

My father said, 'I've got two boys and they're both bloody fools. One plays in a pop group and the other's a Master of Fox Hounds; he's the bigger bloody fool of the two.'

It is my custom during the lambing season to take to my armchair after luncheon and indulge in a little deep thought. My musings the other day were interrupted by the Editor peremptorily demanding an immediate article on Shows.

'But, sir,' I said (well, what else should I call him?) 'have a heart. I am up most of every night.' Well, my dear, you simply will not believe what he said then: I suppose it comes from mixing with all that rough crowd in El Vinos and hunting in Sussex, both experiences liable to coarsen a man. Any road, to the Show.

On the whole, I dislike shows, be they hound, horse, agricultural, fur, feather, or any combination or permutation thereof, but being a man in my position, it is sometimes incumbent upon me to attend one of these orgies of mass misery. Therefore, let us, gentle reader, give them some attention.

Puppy Shows are only as good as the luncheon. I resolutely refuse to attend any Puppy Show where I am not invited to luncheon beforehand. Some determined attention to the browsing and sluicing, if it is of the required standard (high), enables one to endure for the umpteenth time Colonel Potleigh's story of how he felt a little sikh whilst pig sticking in India. Sufficient consumption should also supply enough anaesthetic to enable one to slumber gently under the panama hat throughout the dreary wastes of the judging and awake refreshed in time for the tea. This scheme also makes it possible to avoid perjuring your soul should your host ask you for an opinion on his young hounds. You simply say that you were very impressed with the ones you saw. Mind you, there is no nonsense like that at my Puppy Show: I have a long stick with a spike on the end and everyone sits to, and pays, attention: I will not cast my pearls before swine.

Horse Shows and all equestrian events are the pits. Happily our marriage has not reached the state where Mrs James has to sublimate her desires by breeding Dartmoor ponies. I know men whose summers are rendered hideous by the show circuit. It matters little what the lady wife is into. It may be that she dons a dreadful tweed cap with a pom-pom on it, and a pair of pretty unsuitable corduroy trousers, and is away with the Dartmoor Pony Set (a pretty fast lot, I believe) or, perhaps, an In Hand Hunter, whatever that is, and I do not like the sound of it much. Worst of all, the lady may take up side saddle, and I am here to tell you that that produces some very strange habits indeed.

The lot of the show widower is not an enviable one. On the rare occasions that the lady wife puts in an appearance at the old homestead, she will spend most of her time in bed and a filthy temper. Should he catch a glimpse of her at a show, she will be in stretch jods and a filthy temper.

The show widower may find difficulty in fitting in his job

during the showing season. He will either have the children dumped in his lap ('I'm sorry darling, but I must take Bridget with me. Surely you can cope with the smalls, just for a couple of days.' 'Oh Daddy, not fish fingers again'), or he will be ordered to get off his butt and get to the show, and help.

If you wander round the lorry park at any show, you will see plenty of show widowers. They are sad creatures festooned with rugs, bottles of liniment, tail bandages, martingales, body brushes, and with at least two screaming children, who either want ice creams, or to go, or both simultaneously. It is your Christian duty to ease the lot of these wretched creatures; go up and tell him that his wife has just been put bottom of her class; go on, spread a little happiness.

Terrier Shows are rarer than they used to be, which is good. In the early days they were low key and fun and no one took them terribly seriously. A few years ago I judged a terrier show 'somewhere in the south of England'. Now I like old-fashioned terriers, narrow but with enough leg to run with hounds a bit; most of the terriers at the show had chests like a no 19 bus, and Chippendale legs. The stewards shovelled them out of the ring by the sackful at my behest. Now it transpired that one of the Chippendales was a multi champion, and his proud owner had *flown* him down from Huddersfield, or some such unlikely place, to clean up, only to see his pride and joy slid out on its ear. He protested, he ululated, his muckers (all good Chippendale men) joined in; I was booed, and chiacked from the ringside. I sought harbour in the Secretary's tent where we drank a restoring whisky whilst a harassed assistant kept the howling mob at bay. All in all, it was a splendid sporting occasion, but I have never been asked to judge there again.

I seldom attend Agricultural Shows. I find little pleasure in sitting in a queue of traffic for two hours to get in, secure in the knowledge that I shall have to suffer the same purgatory to get out. Whilst I am there, I always buy something that I had no intention of buying. The trouble is that I am a sucker for gadgets, and an agricultural show is nothing if not full of gadgets. I

always start by buying a patent screwdriver, but this merely whets the appetite and sets me up for a multi-directional drafting gate that enables you to direct a sheep in four directions at once; from this it is only a short step to the multi-sprocketed, flange-adjusted tractor with a built-in sauna bath. That is why I seldom attend Agricultural Shows, that and warm beer in plastic mugs.

I suspect that when the Editor ordered this article, he really had Hound Shows in mind.

A very senior and revered MFH once said to me that he considered that the only useful purpose hound shows served was to enable him to meet his friends. I agree absolutely, the only difference being that I have not got any friends, not after this article.

I think showing hounds is all right, provided that the competitors keep a sense of proportion. Some people take the whole thing much, much too seriously. The official line is that it is good for people to go to shows and to see the high standards of canine pulchritude that can be achieved, and so not to be under an illusion that their geese might be swans. This is a very good point, but what if the search for beauty is conducted at the expense of working qualities? Quite impossible? Unheard of? Heaven preserve your innocence, my son. One of the reasons for the decline of the foxhound during the latter part of the last century and the beginning of this was the rise in influence of Peterborough Show. Hound shows, like whisky, are good in moderation.

I love maps; they provide me with hours of pleasure. In fact, in my advancing years that, a pipe of tobacco, and my weekly milk stout are the only pleasures left to me.

The other day I invested some of my hard-won gelt in the *Ordnance Survey Atlas of Great Britain* and I am already reaping a considerable return in enjoyment, especially when it comes to place names.

I refer mainly to English place names. When it comes to our Celtic and Gaelic cousins I frankly do not know my ABHAINN AN T-STRATH CHUILEANNAICH from my LLANSANTFFRAED-CWM DEUDDWR, but I hope that they both get over it soon. I did notice LEVISHIE FOREST in the north of Scotland which may go to prove that the Scots are indeed the lost tribe of Israel.

Place names can be very evocative. For instance, if you had been living at STARVEALL, SOURHOPE or HUNGRY LAW, no one could really blame you if you finished up at BLUBBERHOUSES and probably went on the SAUCE in a big way.

I regret to say that drink figures largely in English nomenclature, though why we should resort to FRENCH BEER, I do not know; it is very inferior stuff. I am sure one gets better tack at BEERCROCOMBE, but I hope that they drink it prettily with the little finger extended and do not GLOUP it down.

I do not know what a CRASK OF AIGAS tastes like so I think I will stick to CRUG – but in moderation; I do not want to become known as a DRUNKENDUB.

It will probably be wise to suck a MINTO when you have DUNDREGGAN and are heading home to the little woman, or

WIFE GEO; well, whatever turns you on, man. Of course you could try taking her some RED ROSES, and I wish I could work WHAM in here, but in the circumstances it seems pretty unlikely.

However, it is quite certain that after all this boozing you will need a LEEK; if it turns out to be a WYRE PIDDLE then I suggest you consult your doctor at once.

Your GP could be quite a busy man if you insist on a MEALL A' MHUIC. And for goodness sake go steady on the RHUM and EIGG or you will certainly get the dreaded RINNS OF ISLAY.

I should imagine the PRATTS BOTTOM (if you are a private patient, it is called EARL'S SEAT) could be very NASTY indeed. If you dash into the surgery screaming OH ME EDGE, your weary doctor will say that he warned you it would never get well if you PICKET PIECE and now he will have to rub it with SALINE, or if he is a good old-fashioned sort he might well use SPITTAL OF GLENSHEE.

I regret to say that violence crops up from time to time and it is hardly surprising if the inhabitants of MOREBATTLE, BLOODYBUSH and BLOODY HAUGH, NEEDS LAW; in fact, when they have DUNROBIN CASTLE, MEIKLE SAYS LAW very firmly. Meikle will probably consult the old-established law firm of PRIVETT, PROBUS and PRONCY who will certainly brief that eminent Q.C., Mr BANCHORY-DEVENICK and SHOP the lot of them to the fuzz.

I fear our Security Services are in a PETTYMUK again. The infamous HERMA NESS has managed to smuggle MOSCOW into the country and set it up near Kilmarnock. She is known to be planning a clandestine GERMANSWEEK, but I am sure our brave lads in MI6 will put off their bridge tournament and STOB AN T'SLUICHD; that will teach the SWINE, although I think it is a bit near the knuckle to refer to her as the SOW OF ATHOL.

Talking about pigs, there must be a lot of them at TOLLER PORCORUM.

EASTON IN GORDANO is the home of one of those peculiar games like Nurdling and Dwile Flunking.

This game is played with a BIX which you have to CLETT ARD: if you do, you get a LÙB SCORE; if you do not, it is a MINNIGAFF and then you LOSSIT. In this event, all the jolly villagers seize you by your appendages and drop you in SOTS HOLE no matter how much you PRAZE-AN-BEEBLE about it.

All of this may make you think that I am a bit of a WAG; alternatively you may thank GOTT that this article has ended.

(P.S. If you want to know where all these places are, buy the *Atlas* and find them yourselves; I did.)

What a dashing time it is in the north in August.

I used to hate August in the south. I always thought it a sullen month, full of thunder, flies and hound exercise, with very little to relieve the tedium. But in the frozen north, my dear, we are terribly, terribly gay. Four puppy shows, including our own, and Rydal Show, all within ten days. And then in the latter half of the month, cubhunting, and Bellingham and Pennymuir Shows. It is a wonder that any work gets done at all, but it does; and I managed to get my first draw of fat lambs this week.

To Rydal then, with Mrs James and the Senior Joint-Masters, with our tackety boots and horn heid sticks. What fun we had, with everybody whipping bottles out of their cars at an instant's notice. I put Mrs James in for the entered bitches, and entered the Senior Joints for the brace class in the sheepdog trials, but they all failed to win prizes.

I watched the foxhounds being judged by a fat man from the West Percy and a lean man from the VWH. Much to my disappointment, they were not lynched by the spectators after the judging. I have always understood that this good old custom was one of the high spots of the show. However, I gather that, sadly, it has had to be discontinued as it contravenes some obscure section of the Meat (Sterilization and Staining) Regulations Act 1982. It is surely bureaucratic nonsense to interfere with simple rustic pleasure in such a way.

Anyway I bought a terrier, scrounged a few more drinks; then it was back in the chara, with our trousers legs rolled up and knotted handkerchiefs on our heads. The Senior Joint broke out the brown ale and we had community singing all along Hadrian's Wall.

This article is to have a lot about cubhunting in it: I am sorry about that but there it is: those are my instructions, and all of you out there who were hoping for a cosy bit about crochet work and my Great Granny Penhaligon's recipe for camomile tea will just have to preserve your souls in patience.

Sir Valentine Knox considered cubhunting a very moderate amusement compared with shooting. After all, 'No one expects you to shoot before daybreak.' What an effete lot shooters are. Not only can they not get up in the morning but they also stop for lunch in so-called shooting huts where their every whim is catered for in almost Byzantine luxury. After the port, scenes of appalling lubricity take place with all the baser lusts catered for. It is small wonder that all shooters of my acquaintance are overweight and dyspeptic.

Sir Valentine Knox is a secondary character in the *Irish R.M.* stories by Somerville and Ross. If you know and love these stories, I wonder if you were as horrified as I was by the crass and brutal way they were disfigured in that television series. I would like to send the director beating for one of our local shoots: after lunch.

Now then where was I? Ah yes, cubhunting. We have started after a fashion in some of our wilder hill country. This is so remote that there is a twice-weekly mule train, and a chap I met in a cloud on the top of Bloodybush Edge asked me if I was Mr Lloyd George, as he had voted Liberal last time. The Senior Joints have armed guards on the stables with orders to shoot me on sight. So it is tackety boots and motor bicycles.

In previous despatches I have alluded to the shepherding bicycle. It is a vital piece of equipment to the modern hill shepherds, allowing them to herd much larger areas than would have been possible in the foot and pony days. They whizz about the hills with deceptive ease, but then they do it every day; I do not. I came to a conclusion a long time ago that I was not a born horseman (no one disagrees), and I have swiftly come to the conclusion that I am a pretty good muff on a motor bicycle. What is more they know it; they sneer when I approach. As soon as I get in the saddle they either sulk and refuse to start; or, having put themselves craftily in gear, they jam their throttles wide open, rear up like a piece of fried bread, and having deposited me on my bum, they either gallop off across the hill, bucking and cavorting, or turn and rend soft portions of my anatomy with their handlebars. If my bike gets too nappy, I shall just tie the beggar to a bush and stump off on my own. So if you are in the hills this autumn and a stray shepherding bike follows you home, it will be mine; you can tell by the horn case on the handlebars.

So all and all, I tend to spend a lot of my time on my big boots. In theory this is fine because, having dropped on your litter of cubs, all you do is stand on the skyline, wound about with terriers, and lean picturesquely on your horn heid stick while the action takes place in the huge bracken beds below. Occasionally you may ululate; this does absolutely no good at all except to indicate to the assembled public (all four) that you are nominally in control of the proceedings.

In practice, things are not so straightforward. In practice, you wade through 500 acres of neck-high bracken accompanied by 1000 admiring flies. You do not find the cubs because they have packed their buckets and spades and gone to the seaside for the day. *But* you do find smelly, old Grandpa who is looking after things at home, and he knows exactly what it is all about. He does what he always does, he heads for the Tall Timber. The Tall Timber is four miles and three valleys away and covers 7000 acres. Hounds stream away towards the first crest (1500ft) and the hill fog that has been waiting for just the right moment now blots everything out. As James trudges off into misty oblivion, he hears one of his erstwhile companions, heading for home and breakfast, say, 'Ah well, we shan't need him again whilst Tuesday.'

So you see that cubhunting on the hills is not quite what it is in the Blankshire Vale. But it is doing the James wind and figure no end of good. Next week if I am very very good, eat all my cabbage, and get a good chit from Mrs James for conjugal performance, the Senior Joints may, and I stress the *may*, allow me to ride one of my horses. Oh golly! Gosh! Super!

The phrase 'the Opening Meet' will produce many different responses from different people: everything from the keenest anticipation to the bluest, bowel diluting funk. The certain thing is that no one remotely connected with hunting can ignore the Opening Meet, the start of yet another season and therefore a milestone in the life of every hunting person.

Even the local shooting syndicate will be infected by the prevailing excitement, and will telephone the Master the night before the meet to say that they intend to 'stick in' a day, the next day, and shoot all the coverts in the middle of the draw. The Master will thank them politely for their cooperation through gritted teeth, and put the telephone down to find that his wives, children, dogs and the stranger within his gates have all departed separately, severally and at great speed, for outer darkness.

So the great day will dawn. There will be tantrums in the Kennels, and vapours in the stables. The best coat and breeches will have shrunk in some inexplicable way. There are muddy paw marks on the mirror-like boots, and the terrier puppy is quietly chewing the beautifully boned spur straps. The breakfast will burn. The sheep will get out. A man will call to sell you a vacuum cleaner. Throughout the morning, you will be conscious of a nasty knot in the stomach. It does not improve much when you arrive at the meet.

For many people, it will be their first glimpse of a foxhound since the end of last season. Indeed, there will be those unfortunates who will be so trapped by the crush in the bar of the local hostelry that they will be denied any sight of the proceedings outside. Thwarted of the sole purpose of their being there, they tend to become very tired and emotional.

I rather doubt whether any Master and/or huntsman enjoys the Opening Meet. It marks the end of the cubhunting, the private time, that every Master/huntsman must enjoy when he has to please no one but himself and his hounds. From November onwards, he is in the hot seat and has to prove to his followers that he is worthy of the privilege of continuing to spend his money for their benefit.

The Opening Meet, like Boxing Day is a show day. There will be more vehicles than a Panzer *gruppen* and more people than a pop concert; horses will be overfed and over-fresh; nerves will be highly polished and most riders will be clean and slightly oiled.

Twenty separate people will bustle importantly up to the Master and ask him where he is going to draw first.

Ten separate fools will ask him where he is going to finish.

A bewildered lady who has come from the Quorn, and wishes that she hadn't, will ask him where he is going to stop for lunch – actually they call it 'second horses' but what is in a euphemism?

The lady from the local press will ask him if the hounds all have names, and does he know them all? (Cynical smirks from the hunt staff.) The press photographer will be asking if the hounds could be put in a nice straight line.

A man with a beard will come and tell him he is a 'cruel f——'

The Hunt Chairman's lorry will break down in the middle of the road.

The milk tanker will want to come through.

Six rolling-eyed point-to-pointers, festooned in red ribbons, will try to ride their equally highly-strung horses through the middle of hounds.

The man with the tray of drinks will by-pass the hunt staff yet again.

Someone will come up to say that he has just seen men with guns going into the first draw.

The Hon Sec, who should be collecting the cap, is sitting outside the pub with a happy smile and a definite list to port (ruby, non vintage).

All in all, the Opening Meet can be a stern test of nerve and stamina. In fact, the whole thing is sheer hell, but I would not miss it for a free run in a bonded warehouse – I think.

My brother-in-law (may his shadow never grow less) is not only a famous MFH, but also an increasingly notorious starlet on the box. He tends to appear in those scorching domestic dramas where the young squire is carving a round off the housemaid, whilst his sister is doing convoluted things in the landau with the second coachman. At some time in the series there will be a meet at the big house and there you will see the brother-in-law and his hounds hiding behind a vast, false walrus moustache. On occasion he even has a speaking part, and has some immortal prose written for him; lines such as: 'Hounds, gentlemen please' and, 'Who is that bloody woman?' which must be frightfully difficult for him. However, he manages most awfully well, and quite rightly rakes in vast piles of gold for his labours.

The B-i-L is very interesting about the actual filmmaking and particularly about the fox. There is always a shot of a fox having it away on its toes in the hunting scene.

Now you and I have always naively supposed that the

director lets a camera team out of its cage and says: 'Go get me some shots of a running fox and don't come back until you have them.' Not a bit of it: all those foxes are paid up Equity members. In fact, in a recent drama in which the B-i-L figures largely (and I use the word advisedly), no less than five foxes were auditioned for the part. Now this blows the mind, and one imagines queues of stage-struck foxes all ready with a pithy piece from *Hamlet,* or a touch of the Lady Bracknells. However, I think it only fair to warn all would-be vulpine thespians that my hounds watch television somewhat infrequently, and that any fox, however famous, should not assume that the hounds are only after its autograph.

A friend of mine was also involved in the making of a historical drama; his part consisted of walking about with a couple of lurchers looking mediaeval. On his way home his journey took him through the local hunt's scene of operations. An obviously well-hunted fox crossed the road and, sportsman that he is, what could be more natural than to leap out of his car and wave his hankie. He said afterwards that the huntsman looked rather bemused but then it is not every day that a huntsman receives information about his hunted fox from a heavily-cowled monk.

Yet another story from the world of showbiz. A

certain hunt, that shall remain nameless in the interests of propriety, agreed to pose as the background for some modelling pictures. There they were, all drawn up at the Opening Meet whilst in the foreground a nubile nymphette, in hunting clothes, was being photographed in a variety of interesting poses. Very good you say, so what? Ah ha my masters, here's the rub. No sooner had the hunt departed than the gel started to strip, being as it were Play Bunny of the Month or some such!

All this suggests a somewhat disturbing trend in my opinion. Are we to see MsFH signing up with model agencies? Or the committee of the MFHA doing a song-and-dance routine to advertise chocolate-covered wafer biscuits? Where will it all end, I ask myself? However, if anyone is interested, I am prepared to let the advertising space on the backs of the hunting coats of our Hunt Chairman and Hon Sec; both would accommodate a fair-sized poster.

There are those who consider that selling your Hunt Chairman as a hoarding, or posing with naked starlets, or even being photographed in a false moustache are not suitable pastimes for an MFH. They might even be classed as 'Conduct Unbecoming ...' It has been made fairly clear to me that writing for magazines is regarded as 'Conduct Unbecoming' in certain quarters. Indeed, there is a fundamentalist view that an ability to read and write at all should preclude anyone from becoming an MFH. I must admit that when you see some of the things that MsFH write, then you can see the fundamentalist point of view.

Are your hounds steady on wolves or wallabies? I do not suppose that you have the least idea. I remember a big scare when a wallaby escaped from a wildlife park into the next day's draw. I was secretly disappointed that we never found it. They hunt them in Tasmania, but I have no idea what sort of point you get with a wallaby.

I do know that my hounds are not steady on wolves. Some

years ago, hounds split and five couple disappeared over a nasty uncrossable river; the terrier Land-Rover was sent in pursuit. The hounds took a lot of finding having made a 5-mile point into a neighbouring country and also, as it happened, into a wildlife park.

In the middle of the wildlife park was a large enclosure that contained a small pack of depressed and somewhat scabious wolves which spent their days scratching and thinking about the good old days on the Tundra. Their deliberations were disturbed by the arrival of my missing five couple who, having lost their fox downwind of the hippo, were casting diligently about until they happened upon the wolves. Now I very much doubt that any of those hounds had ever seen a wolf before but there was instant recognition that here was something that very definitely required hunting. When the terrier van arrived and spoilt the fun, the wolves were going very fast round the *inside* of the enclosure, with the hounds in full cry on the *outside*. So if anybody has a lupine problem, just drop me a line. I have the only hounds in Great Britain entered to wolf.

I have always understood that the last wild wolf in England was killed in the reign of the first Elizabeth, but they survived in Scotland into the 1600s when a bounty was offered on the corpses of 'Wolves and Tories'.

In case you should think that this was a slogan devised by some sort of seventeenth-century Militant Tendency, I should point out that the word 'Tory' is derived from the Gaelic word 'Toraidhe', meaning a thief. I am amazed that no Labour politician has yet latched on to this fact, but now the Chancellor has put up the price of my whisky and tobacco again, I shall supply the information to the Welsh *x* Scottish leader of the Opposition, free gratis and for nothing.

We have quite a lot of forestry plantations in our country and get hounds with nasty rips from the top strand of barbed wire. Did you know that barbed wire was invented by a woman? There is a rich psychological vein there waiting to be mined. Young hounds are especially prone to these injuries until they learn the technique of 'banking' the fences.

While looking at one of these wounds the other day, I remembered a West Country reservoir that is entirely surrounded by a fence of spiked iron railings which runs for some miles. Before Hitler's war some hounds got impaled on these railings and the MFH sent out a blacksmith and had a metal knob put on every spike. I am not contemplating doing the same thing on our barbed wire fences; I just wish that wretched woman had stuck to crochet work.

I was involved in an attempted rape in the hunting field the other day. Now we do not actually get a lot of that sort of thing, although the Vice-Chairman did not get his position by playing tiddly-winks. The facts of the case are these, m'lud. It was a bad scenting day and hounds had checked and were casting busily but without effect. I was sitting on my mare, looking varminty and praying for a holloa while the field were wittering in the background. Suddenly the mare erupted in a paroxysm of squealing and kicking and I looked round to find a gert big cart colt climbing aboard with a grin on his face, and lust on his mind. Well, my dear, what does one do! I mean for all I knew having ravished the mare, the brute might keep climbing and start on me; it was all just too, too much. So I belted the bleeder round the lug, and the mare gave him the old one, two in his left luggage. The last I saw, he was sitting down clutching his testimonials with a pained expression on his face and serve him jolly well right.

So take heed all of you, and be told: the Old Mare and I will not be molested out hunting. However, I am open to offers outside office hours: form an orderly queue, and no garlic, please.

One of the happiest side effects from the finish of hunting is the sudden silence of the magisterial telephone. All through the season the apparatus crouches in its corner, like some malevolent minor deity. It is just as demanding too, ringing constantly at meal times, bath times, during the telly serial of the moment, and just as you are drifting off to sleep. An MFH is a public figure and shall be required at all times to be available at the end of the telephone to be abused, cajoled, bullied and bored to distraction all of which he must accept with the best possible grace.

Mrs James is a slave to the telephone, shooting up like a pheasant at the slightest tinkle. I am more hardened in my sin; I either refuse to answer it or say that I am 'The Stenning Steam Laundry'. The moral of this is that if you want to abuse, cajole or bully me, do not waste your time and mine telephoning but send a man with a message in a cleft stick – it will have just as much effect!

4

'What?' people ask me, 'what do you do when you finish hunting? I suppose you have a lovely easy time.' Heaven preserve their innocence. As soon as hunting finishes, I plunge headlong into the maelstrom of lambing. This year Dame Nature played a merry jape on me and triggered the reproductive process ten days early – and, no, I had not got my dates muddled. This meant that the end of hunting and the beginning of lambing overlapped, which is not a happy situation.

However, we got through it and life is almost back to normal, although it has to be said that those accustomed to the round, jolly, MFH who has spent all season spreading sweetness and light along the southern edge of the Cheviots would hardly recognize the other James. Alas, no, the James of the merry quip and the toothpaste ad smile, on the placid surface of whose personality no slight ripple has been detected throughout a long hard season, has gone. In his place is a red-eyed, unshaven, rawboned Mr Hyde whose high explosive content is on a two-second fuse.

So what other hoops will our handsome hero have to jump through before he can once again strap the horn case on the saddle?

The next thing to be faced is *the holiday*. Holidays are not my strong point. My idea of R & R is my armchair, a book and a pipe, but Mrs James is strong on AWAY. It is in vain that I point out that we go to Peterborough Royal Foxhound Show every year which involves two nights' absence from home. If I am really brave I point out that she also has the pleasure of going shopping in Alnwick every week which entails my getting my own lunch. It is all to no avail, I have to go to Spain. This is not as bad as it might be because my mother now lives in Spain and so I simply transfer my pipe and book to one of her armchairs. But it is a long way to go to do it.

'Getting there,' some twit said, 'is half the fun.' He never envisaged travelling on a charter flight to Alicante. If animals at the Mart were treated like charter flight passengers, there would be prosecutions, fines, imprisonment and strong words from the bench, and rightly so. As far as comfort goes, the seats are passable if you are 5ft 3in like Mrs James, but it is the Quart and the Pint Pot as far as I am concerned. However, we finally arrived at Alicante and Mother was there to rescue us from the rest of the passengers who were formed into chain gangs and taken away to Benidorm.

There are foxes in Spain, because there is a stuffed one in a restaurant where we often go. It is a miserable little thing, about the size of a poorish tomcat. I cannot believe that Spain is a good scenting country but there is a pack of hounds, somewhere outside Marbella which has a sizeable British colony. I have seen a picture of them in the *Costa Brava News*, but it is too far away for me to be bothered to go and investigate. (It is boring enough having to look at all my friends' hounds in England.) I wonder if the Royal Calpe hounds still exist, down near Gibraltar? There is certainly plenty of space in Spain for hunting where the booze is cheap even if the foxes are small.

One of the great pleasures that foxhunters look forward to in the summer is meeting again their far-flung acquaintances. Time and logistics make it difficult to stray far from one's patch during the winter months. I rarely even find time to have a day with my near neighbours. In fact, I hardly ever leave my rock-bound, mist-sodden lair, where Mrs James sits stirring the cauldron, and dreeing her weird as they say up here. If you are wondering how to do it, my advice to you is not to bother too much; I should leave your weird undreed.

Now where was I? Ah yes; meeting the chums. This is the great pleasure of the summer shows, because quite frankly when you have seen one hound/horse/heifer you have seen them all. I know that there are a lot of tense ladies in stretch jods and Herpes scarves, who spend all summer showing ponies when they ought to be ministering to the needs of their husbands and children. There are also men, and women, who would go to hound shows six days a week, and sit there sucking their pencils and looking knowledgeable, dreaming of good second thighs and stamina points (on hounds of course).

But these, my dears, are the lunatic fringe, the Militant Tendency of the hound/horse world. Horses and hounds are for pursuing and catching the fox, they have no other purpose.

Shows are for the crack: they have no other purpose. It is great fun getting all the gossip and the scandal. I am always interested to see who has traded in their spouse for a newer and sportier model.

It is sad to note how much fatter all my friends have got in the last year, and what a terribly expensive nose Bertie is getting.

Poor Amethyst has fallen all abroad, and just look at that frightful hat: her taste in hats is about as good as her taste in men.

Old George says that he has had a cracking season, but Charley told me that George's nerve has gone and they have to pull every fence down for him. Bill says that Charley is totally enslaved by the large moustached lady who does the knackering . . . and so it goes on.

The fact of the matter is that foxhunters are a jealous lot. Every Master/huntsman thinks that he is *the man*. He is certain that his methods and his hounds are the only ones, and that everybody else is a fool and a charlatan. You try telling your MFH what a wonderful hunt you had with one of his neighbours and he will sink his fangs in your jugular. Therefore it follows that no MFH ever wants to hear good news about another MFH. When he asks you how young/old so-and-so is getting on at the Blankshire, he wants you to purse your lips, click your teeth, and shake your head, and my advice to you is to do it, otherwise he will sugar off and let you pay for the lunch. So off you go to the shows and have a good gossip; there is nothing like a few scurrilous stories, but on the way home, just reflect a moment and ask yourself what all your friends have been saying about *you*.

I got my first fan letter the other day from a nice lady in Kiribati. You will be as mystified as I am as to the whereabouts of Kiribati, and all I can tell you is that it is in the Central Pacific, which pin-points it exactly, and it does not sound as though the hunting is very good there. But is it not exciting to think that *Shooting Times* reaches even unto the farthest corners of the globe, and refreshes the parts that other magazines cannot reach? Perhaps I shall become a cult figure in the Pacific and when the Kiribatics are not ironing their grass skirts they will sacrifice the odd virgin to the Great White Writer Over the Sea. On second thoughts, chaps, if you do have any odd virgins, hang onto them until I come; all same like King Victoria.

The Game Fair: now is not that an exciting thought? It is most unfortunate that I shall be indisposed this year and so be unable to attend. In fact I intend to be indisposed every year at Game Fair time, so will everybody please note that I shall not be available, this year, next year, or ever again.

I have only been to the Game Fair once. It was all the Black Colonel's fault; he insisted that I form part of a 'Forlorn Hope' of MsFH to man a stand that was intended to prove that pheasants did not eat foxes and vice versa. Well you cannot refuse the Black Colonel for he is a Very Important Person. It is thought that he spends his time leaning on a halberd guarding a Very Important Thunderbox to see that it is vacant for Even More Important People, and is not, at crucial moments, full of itinerant Irish labourers, Liverpudlian buskers, tired and emotional cabinet ministers, and all other such human flotsam who apparently throng the passages of Very Important Places of Residence. So you see, when such a man says jump, you jump and of course I did.

Getting in was great fun. Nothing adds more zest to a day than sitting for two hours in a queue for somewhere you were not nuts about going to in the first place. It was as I thought it would be. Came lunch-time and everybody sugared off to sample the lucullan delights of the CLA tent, followed by a session of ribaldry and mirth amongst the rare vintages of the *Shooting Times*.

But what of I? I was left tethered to a stake in the tent, with a bottle of Newcastle Brown (flat) and two cheese sandwiches on permanent loan from British Rail (E. Region). There I stayed, howling dismally, the whole afternoon whilst large men in shot-proof Harris tweed, and impenetrable Scottish accents, argued as to how much my pelt would fetch.

In view of all this, you will not expect to see me in the

queue this year; Gunmakers' Row will know me not (they do not anyway) and the Country Landowners will chill the Krug in vain. James will not be there; in fact I come all over queer at the thought of it. I do hope you all enjoy yourselves quite enormously.

I have a friend who is Big in Television (I think he works the clouds in the weather forecast) and at one stage of his career he was with Backwoods Television. He describes the Directors of Backwoods as people who spent all summer catching salmon, and all winter eating them in velvet smoking jackets (the Directors, that is, not the salmon); indeed, I find it very heartening to know that there are still Directors like that. I thought that they were all two-button jackets and phony suntans these days.

Any road, one summer the Board was discussing Names for a spectacular show with my friend advising. One Household Name in particular was favoured by the Board. 'Not so,' said my friend. 'I happen to know that he is shooting at Elstree at the moment.' The Board considered this in a rather puzzled fashion, until at last an eminent Backwoodsman asked, 'But what the hell is the feller shooting at this time of year?' There you are. You can all tell each other that story in the queue for the Game Fair.

To London, for the annual shirt. I am not keen on London. As a young man I spent four miserable years as an underpaid serf in a Dickensian office in the City. Jermyn Street is the only place where I can buy shirts that will encompass the manly James form and which will do up at the collar without garrotting me. The James shape is distinctive and baffles most people. In fact, a year or two back an eminent firm of country clothiers took up a challenge of mine and undertook to 'clothe me from head to foot': as yet they have failed to come up to scratch. However, Jermyn Street swathes the manly James torso in cotton, and encompasses the large James feet in toe-capped leather, and even supplies the latest member of the bow tie stable, at a price admittedly, but without hesitation.

All so unlike the provinces where people suck their teeth, and call me 'squire' and tell me, 'There is no call for that sort of thing these days, but we can do you a 17in neck in pure terri-propi-crumplene' when I have asked for a 18½ in white cotton.

I saw an unusual sight in Jermyn Street this year. The shadows were lengthening and I was promenading in leisurely fashion towards the club, with tea and toast foremost in the mind. I was at peace with the world on the whole, although I was slightly worried that I had my braces perhaps an inch too long, thereby spoiling the hang of the well-cut trousers over the highly polished shoes (these things loom large in a chap's life). It was then I saw the unusual sight. The first thing I noticed was a pair of hound-stained corduroy trousers, and I know hound-stained trousers when I see them. Below the trousers were a pair of stout, tackety shoes, whilst above they merged into a tattered tweed coat, from which there stuck out the well-pinned throttle, and the purple, perspiring face of a well-known and much-loved northern MFH. The whole thing was moving at a brisk hand canter and causing not a little stir amongst the solid burghers there present.

'Just going for a haircut,' he boomed as he shot past me. A likely story! I only hope that his lovely wife never gets to hear of it.

I am a Cornishman and like most exiles I view the place where I was bred and buttered with a certain nostalgia, coupled with the conviction that the place has gone badly downhill since I graced it by living there. The 'Delectable

Duchy' has probably suffered more than most parts of Britain from invasion by foreigners.

I think I had better qualify that statement in case it is read by one of the battered mandarins from the Foreign Office. I do not want that worthy starting from his well-upholstered chair with a modulated, strangled cry under the impression that the old firm has bungled yet again, and that Colonel Gaddafi has taken over Penzance when no one was looking; we do not want the Special Boat Squadron disrupting the cloistered calm of the Royal Fowey Yacht Club, do we?

For the purposes of this exercise, 'foreigner' means anybody who comes from north of the Tamar. It is a very real invasion. Whole Cornish villages are now entirely populated by geriatric refugees from Selly Oak and Macclesfield. Spokespersons for Mabion Kernow proclaim Cornish nationalism in the rich accents of deepest Ruislip.

The takeover has been very marked in the farming world. For a long time, land in Cornwall was comparatively cheap, and thus it became a repository for agricultural oddballs and misfits of every shape, size and description.

I was discussing this problem with a grand old man who was for many, many years the presiding genius at a famous Cornish foxhound kennels. His rule of thumb was simple. If the cattle in the fields ahead were red South Devons, then kick on. However, if there were what he called 'coloured cows' in the field, then look out for squalls. What he meant was that the South Devons were likely to be owned by natives, and the others were likely to indicate troublesome foreigners.

I was mulling this over on the tractor the other day, and I came to the conclusion that it is very possible for an MFH to form a broad idea of what to expect by looking over the hedge. As this is the time of year when pink and shining new Masters are setting out in their little vans, with hope in their hearts and a sandwich in their pockets, to 'get round the country' (poor little bleeders), allow me to offer the 'James Early Warning Guide'.

It may be that your hunting country is wall-to-wall winter

corn and the only living things in it are pheasants. If this is the case, do not despair; not yet, you will have all season to do that in. My advice is plenty of cold baths, vigorous exercise, and keep putting the powder in your tea.

However, let us suppose that you have at least one farm in your country with livestock. Now take a careful peep over the hedge. What do you see? Channel Island cows and/or goats; props, Miss Lettuce and Miss Parsley. Oh dear! Well, quite frankly you are better off with the winter corn and the pheasants.

I think that it was the 9th Duke of Beaufort who encouraged his tenants to keep the old Gloucester cattle, which I believe to be now extinct. Not only were they good milkers (Double Gloucester cheese), but so placid in temperament that they took no notice at all of the passing of the ducal hounds.

I am not going to get too involved with the virtues and vices of different breeds of cattle and resultant correspondence with herd book secretaries. Let me just say that sensible people tend to keep sensible stock. It is the exotics, two- and four-legged, you have to be wary of. Pretty sound all-round advice I call that.

The other day I was performing that fascinating, and intellectually satisfying, task generally known as 'crutching out sheep'. Whilst straightening the back and mopping the brow between patients, I noticed an old man leaning on the gate watching me. There is nothing strange in this; I attract old men in the same way that sheep attract blowflies. I will lay you a guinea to a gooseberry that were I to go five miles from the nearest sign of habitation, on a bare hillside, and there start performing some simple agricultural task, within minutes there would be at least two old men leaning on a gate watching me; they even bring their own gates. For the most part they watch in silence, puffing their pipes and, in an occasional display of emotion, spitting. In moments of really high drama they will nudge each other and point with horny fingers, shaking, the while, with suppressed mirth. It makes me wonder whether I should not get myself declared an SSSI and put in for a grant on myself.

Anyway, there was I and there was he, leaning and puffing, so I gave him a civil greeting. He returned my salutation and said that I was cowing sheep. Now this made me prick up my ears for here was a new word, and I just love new words.

'How,' I asked, 'do you spell cow?' He pondered this for a moment and then said: 'You don't spell it, you just say it.'

It seems to me that there is a rich vein waiting to be mined somewhere in there. How many words are there that are never spelt, just said; especially dialect words?

I have always been interested in dialect and accent, and as I have moved from one end of England to the other, I have lived in several different language zones and can claim to be fairly fluent in three or four of them. It seems to me that it is mainly in agriculture and allied trades that the old words remain. It is also rather sad that on the whole they may not survive in everyday use beyond the present generation. But I may be wrong: I was once.

In case I am right I present hereunder a paragraph containing words that are in common use in various parts of the realm, but which, to the best of my knowledge and belief, have never been spelt before:

'The Pharisees' goyle is so wick with dashels that if you go riving about down there with the put you will likely cowp on an emmett but and be hoyed out on your yud.'

('The fairies' glen is alive with thistles and if you go galloping about down there with the cart you will hit an ant hill and be thrown out on your head.')

My current landlord is a great foxhunter and although somewhat stricken by the march of time he is blessed with total recall. He is a mine of fascinating information and gobbits of gossip. The other morning he told me that he had his first morning's cubhunting in 1900. The meet was some eight miles from his home and he rode on. By the end of the morning he was further from home and utterly exhausted, but in the nick of time there appeared his mother in the family victoria (remember them?). The boy was put in the carriage and the pony tied on behind – now you could not do that with a Mini Metro.

I have never been a great enthusiast for hacking home after hunting, probably because I have had to do it in the past. I can find no merit in having influenza half way on a pottery horse, several missing hounds, and ten miles to ride home in the encircling gloom; not a happy thought is it? What is more, it is just starting to snow.

The farthest I can remember riding home was twenty-six miles, and while it is a useful thing to be able to bang on about to the coming generation to prove to them what a load of milk-white little woofters they are, I can say in all honesty that after more than twenty years I can still remember the misery of that ride.

No, that is all in the past for old James. At the end of the day he wants to be rumped up in the lorry cab as quickly as possible, well wrapped in the famous overcoat, and having a good guzzle at the thermos.

Now that I am reviving old memories, it comes to me that

perhaps my most dreadful hack home was completely horseless. I had been out hunting with a foot pack somewhere in the deepest depths of darkest Wales. We had had a good hunt across many miles of trackless mountain, finishing in the dark somewhere between Welshpool and Cardigan Bay. Now, I thought, must be the time to seek out a friendly farmhouse where tea and perhaps a drop of land-of-my-fathers can be had whilst the transport is gathered up. Not a bit of it. We solemnly set out to trudge back over the mountains every blighted mile that we had walked. I was not hill fit like all the others there present, but there was no choice but to keep up; it was a long way to nowhere. I believe that we had walked out about ten miles; it was twenty back.

Whilst we are in the Principality, as it were, I must mention that it was there that I saw a most interesting method of feeding hounds. I was staying with the Master and proprietor and after a very brief acquaintance it had become obvious to him that I was a very great expert in all things canine and vulpine – I had told him so. No doubt suitably impressed, he asked me if I would like to see the hounds fed. Who could refuse such an offer?

Outside the kennels was a large oak tree with a block and tackle secured to one of the branches, and on the hook was the half-eaten carcase of a stirk. The feeding system was extremely simple. The carcase was lowered to the required level; the kennel door flung wide, and the hounds allowed to help themselves to as much as they could reach. When the required intake had been achieved, the corpse was pulled back up into the larder. As a simple feeding method it takes a bit of beating.

There is a well-known West Country kennel that I used to visit a lot at one time. The yards are built in a series of steps on a hillside, and a stream runs from top to bottom through each of the yards. It was quite the easiest kennel to wash down that I have known.

We have started cubhunting about a week later than last year. There was no particular reason for this, except that the cob was not ready before. Last year I started on foot, but the increasingly felt effects of age, vice and unsoundness made me less than eager to repeat that experiment so I bought a cob. The cob is really splendid; a proper *multum in parvo*. Riding him is a bit like sitting on a cricket ball that Mr Botham has just clobbered for six. However, he obviously likes the job, and that is very important for a huntsman's horse.

There has been no question of getting in bye, as yet; most of the winter corn is cut, but some of the spring corn will be a bit of time so we started on a bit of hill not too far from the kennels.

We took all the young hounds. There are different schools of thought on this matter. Some people think it better to introduce the young hounds in stages, a few at a time, and I can see their point of view. But we do not have a big entry and they have all been brought up amongst sheep. It just seems to me that hounds will learn nothing if they are left in the kennels. Whichever way you do it, the first few mornings are always an anxious time for a hill huntsman.

It is good if the young hounds can be settled and hunting a bit before the bracken starts to turn. Bracken carries a bit of scent when it is green, or when it is dead. Whilst it is dying it stinks, and makes hunting extremely difficult. The bracken is nothing like as thick as it was last year and that is a bit of a help. Our bracken beds are vast, and foxes can take some finding, especially if the scent is bad. You know of course where the litters were born, but once the bracken grows, it can be very difficult to keep tabs on them. So far we have been fortunate and have managed to drop on the cubs in fairly short order.

Scent has not been good, so far. The weather has been unsettled. As is usually the case, the two weeks immediately before we started were perfect for cubhunting, still and settled, with good dews in the mornings. As soon as we started, the high pressure moved off to Scandinavia, or some such impossible place, and the lows came sweeping in from the Atlantic – and the Atlantic Lows are such a rough lot; one would hardly ask them to dinner.

However, the mornings that we have had so far have been most useful. There has been a good show of foxes, and we have found at least one litter each morning. There is absolutely no question of holding up on the hills, and the young hounds are thrown in at the deep end, so to speak. All I can say is, so far, so good. None of them is hanging about, and if they are not yet certain what all the fuss and excitement is about, they all seem determined to find out.

There are a lot of roe out on the hill this time, but they have not yet been a problem with the puppies. In fact, we had a bit of luck the other morning: we had hunted, killed, and eaten our fox and were drawing rather vaguely back to the box when a buck jumped up in the middle of hounds and ran right between George and me, allowing us both to point out the error of their ways to those puppies who thought to make whoopee, and to reason with them in a christian spirit.

We do not get too many people out with us as yet. Most of our people are much too busy with corn and/or lambs; at least, that is what they tell me. It is a funny thing, I get people wittering on to me about when am I going to start? They can't wait to be out in the early mornings; and I must be getting old and soft because I have not started. So where are these mad keen people these fine autumn mornings? Rumped up in bed, with the sheets over their heads, that's where they are; as I kenned fine they would be.

I suppose that our most satisfying morning to press was the last one.

It was a stormy morning with squalls and rainbows. Hounds took some time to find, and I know that they missed at least one fox. At last they hit a drag and puzzled it out for a long time, just speaking here and there, with the occasional burst of music. It looked at one time as though they were going right out over the top to where lurk thousands of acres of screaming forest. However, they swung back and niggled over into the Basin, which is a huge natural amphitheatre. Here at last we got into the litter and there was some stirring hunting, with the welkin well and truly ringing.

After a bit they all got together on one fox and bustled away over the top. What scrambling of shepherding bikes, what slithering of Suburus, and through it all the cob and I going uphill like a collective cock pheasant.

When I got round the shoulder I was lucky enough to see hounds coming in, and they checked in a bracken bed right in front of me: silence: then a single hound spoke and there was the fox going away just in front of them: they roared down the hill and disappeared over a brae. The cob and I descended in as dignified a manner as the cob allows and there they were, marking strong in a neat little rabbit hole.

After the appropriate conclusion we hacked back over the hill, through the bonnie purple heather, with the curlews whistling like billyo.

I was conscripted to play cricket for the hunt the other week. It is thirty years since I have touched a cricket bat and to save feverish hammering on my door by the England selectors, it will be quite thirty years before I will consider touching one again. I was not a success. I should have been quite all right in the field had not the batsmen persisted in continually hitting the ball at me. I resented this familiarity. A cricket ball is a nasty hard thing, and when I tried to stop it with my hand, it hurt my fingers. I tried stopping it with my feet and hurt my feet. In the end, if the ball came my way I either ducked, or stepped aside and let it all flow past me; there seemed to be plenty of other people who were only too willing to run after the wretched thing. The only thing that can be said for my batting is that, while I understand that it provoked quite a lot of interesting comment from the spectators, it hardly came up to the high standards that my fielding performance might have led people to expect.

A most extraordinary thing. I called in on a friend who has the enviable task of keeping me supplied with horses. He had just brought a load of garrons down from the north of Scotland, and one of them was an hermaphrodite ('human being, animal, combining characteristics of both sexes'). It really was the most peculiar creature, and if you have never seen one I should not lose too much sleep over it. But, as my friend said, it should always be able to entertain itself.

It occurred to me the other day that my present kennels are the first ones at which I have no livestock. For many years I kept my gamecocks at the kennels; they used to thrive round the flesh house. Then there was a long succession of kennel goats. The most memorable of these was Boris. Boris came as a kid, semi-crippled from being shut in a tiny box; he was destined for the pot, but I thought him worthy of better things. He grew into a strong and healthy goat of extremely forceful character. He never considered himself to be anything other than a hound, and used to walk out, and come on the shorter hound exercise. His proper home was the grassyard which he ruled. No young hound who graduated from Boris's grassyard showed any subsequent desire to interfere with anything on cloven hooves.

Boris was omnivorous. I found him one day with the remnants of a form from the tax office that the postman had only half put through the letter box. I rang the Inland Revenue and explained. They sent me two forms: one for me, and one for the goat.

You can tell that hunting is under way – there is a marked increase in the amount of horse droppings in the road. Perhaps you live in an area where show jumpers and, Heaven help you, polo players have their being, in which case your roads are manured all summer and you will not notice the difference. In this area, people keep horses for hunting, as is quite proper, and the signs are there for all to see.

In this column in the past I have been pretty sour about people who get too enthusiastic about showing their hounds. However, there are different aspects to all things and it behoves fair-minded people to see the other chap's point of view. I have always had my view of hound shows coloured by the fact that my hounds never won any prizes. I am big enough to realize that my outlook has been prejudiced and we took our hounds to the 'Peterborough of the Borders' (or should Peterborough be called the 'Bellingham of the South'?) and won lots of lovely rosettes, including a clean sweep in the unentered bitches.

In the light of this win and the further illumination provided by generous draughts of celebratory whisky, the truth dawned and I saw with startling clarity how important hound shows are. After all, if people like me do not show our hounds, how can lesser mortals ever have a standard of excellence to which to aspire?

A horrid incident at the kennels. Our kennels lie beside a road. It is not a busy road but it does carry a certain amount of holiday traffic in the summer, and during the local rush hour, there can be as many as three cars in half-an-hour. Baxter is being walked at the kennels. I suppose you have guessed what is coming next? A lady rushed into the kennels the other day with an armful of Baxter crying that she had found the poor little thing in the road all covered in blood (cue violins). Baxter seemed remarkably hale and hearty although undeniably red. What had happened was that George's son had found some red paint and a brush, and had decided that rather than a boring old, run of the mill, lemon and white puppy, he would have a red, lemon and white puppy.

My brother returned from a tour of the southern United States not long ago. He stayed for a short time at a small town in the boondocks where the local youth practised a most unusual sport. The town consisted of one long street on a steep hill; at the bottom of the street the road did a sharp right turn with a formidable drop. At the top of the town was a truck stop (transport café to you). The game was quite simple; you went up to the top and cut the brake pipes on the waiting trucks, and then you went down town and bet on how many would make it round the bend. You have to admit it's different and I am rather surprised it did not feature in the Olympics.

Still on foreign travel: on my summer forays to the south I see a lot of towns with foreign 'twins'. Thus you may have Tetbury twinned with Crespigny-sur-Lorne or Banbury twinned with Nizni Novgorod, I should not wonder. I feel sure it is a fine thing for international understanding, and no doubt leads to much junketing that the ratepayers shell out for with a smile on their lips and joy in their hearts.

But there is one set of twins that always fascinates me. If you were to travel from the A1 west to Oakham, it is very likely that you would pass through a village that we will call Whitwell. At a passing glance, Whitwell consists of two farms, perhaps twenty houses, a church, and if there is a public house then I must have missed it. Whitwell is twinned with Paris; it says so on the county council sign, so it must be so.

I assume that it is Paris, France and not Paris, Minnesota, and quite frankly my mind boggles. Even my limited imagination can work out what the Whitwell Parish Councillors do on a fraternal visit to Paris, but what, oh what, does the civic delegation of stout Paris burghers do in Whitwell? One can only hope that the Whitwell Women's Institute is equal to the challenge.

I do not travel any more than I can help and, whenever possible, I travel by train. I have always liked trains and I think that, at its best, it is a most civilized form of travel; unfortunately trains are seldom at their best these days. In the days when I did a lot of rail travel, I never went without a copy of *Baily's Hunting Directory*. I always liked to know exactly whose country I was galloping through, and jumping all the fences in. It is only fair to add that I was much braver behind a Castle Class loco than I ever would have been on a horse.

In the early 1960s I was a Dickensian serf chained to an office stool in the Great Wen. Twice in the year they undid my padlock and sent me to Newcastle upon Tyne, with a keeper, to do an audit. The work was just as dreary as it was in London, but I liked Newcastle which then hadn't had its guts torn out by the developers. I also enjoyed the train journey. As I remember, the early part of the journey, through Cambridgeshire and Nottinghamshire, was plough even in those days. Thirsk was the place that I looked forward to. From the train you could see the splendid escarpment of the

Hambledon Hills and Sutton Bank. I had never been over those hills in body but, with the help of *Baily's,* I knew that over those hills were all sorts of splendid sporting packs who must be longing for a young man strong in back and keenness, if a trifle short in brains and worldly goods.

The country north of Thirsk, then, was a sea of grass, with lovely thorn fences and timber. Now I have lived and hunted beyond those hills, and they are no longer a mystery to me. However, they hold many happy memories, and I still look out for the Hambledons when the train approaches Thirsk, even if they are set in a sea of winter corn today.

In my youth and the days of steam, I was privileged to ride on the footplate from time to time, and I formed a lasting admiration for the footplate-men. The fascination of driving a steam engine is that it is a very difficult thing to do well, and I always thought that the drivers I met were very similar to top class professional huntsmen.

I am not sure that I could award the same accolade to all the current employees of B. Rail. I recently had occasion to travel from west to north. It was very hot and the air conditioning was knackered. The charming Caribbean guard promised repairs at Bristol and then Gloucester. At Birmingham a small man appeared, totally dwarfed by the enormous screwdriver that apparently held him up. He looked at the heating console, tapped it with his screwdriver, sucked his teeth, and broke into a torrent of passionate patois. The guard translated: 'He say he can't touch it without a certificate.'

'Well for goodness sake, get him a certificate,' cried I.

'He never get certificate,' said the guard, contemptuously, 'he only screwdriver man.' So we boiled all the way home. Give more power to the people, brother.

I was reading a piece in the *Daily Telegraph* about the decline of the grouse in Scotland. I do not have any personal stake in the grouse. I do not shoot them, and find them pretty well inedible. It may be that if I ever ate them when they had been cooked I might enjoy them, but it appears that this is not the way to eat them. Whenever kind people have produced grouse for my delectation, they have been red raw, with the consistency of sorbo rubber, and frankly horrid, but perhaps one requires a palate refined on oatmeal and raw whisky to really appreciate the things. But I digress; the thing that really fascinated me in this article was the mention of:

'Sheikh Hamdan Al Maktoum, a Scottish landowner.' I think that this is absolutely splendid, especially as, if you listen to your average Albannach wittering on, you would think that the whole of Scotland was currently owned by the Birmingham Chamber of Commerce.

Now here we have a genuine Sheikh, come to pour his petro-dollars into the great Scottish sporran, which shows that his heart is in the right place, whatever he wears under his kilt.

What about his kilt? I wonder, what tartan does he wear? Hunting Lambert perhaps? But knowing the ingenuity of the Scots when there is a groat to be turned, I prophesy that it will be only a matter of time before some antiquarian unearths the fact that the McToums are in fact a long lost cadet branch of Clan Campbell. I just hope that His Excellency does not get wind of the theory that the Scots are the lost ten tribes of Israel.

Our cubhunting is well under way but, at the time of writing, it has been nothing to write home about. Foxes have turned up well on the whole, but scent has been very poor, and non-existent on some mornings. What is especially galling is that one of my neighbours is having a most exciting time, and is felling foxes right, left and centre, with a screaming scent. His country is very similar to mine and we exist cheek-by-jowl; yet very often, if we get a scent, he does not and vice versa. What a truly strange and unpredictable thing scent is. Anyway I do not for one moment wish my colleague any less scent, but I would like just a bit more for my lot.

The young hounds have done quite well so far and I am cautiously pleased with them. However, they have a long way to go yet. I do not regard a hound as being properly entered until its second opening meet.

My kind friend, Mr Pyrs Williams, has sent me a smashing Welsh whelp. I have never had a pure Welsh hound before, and I shall watch her progress with keen interest. She has the most amazing ears which she somehow never quite treads on. She is called Gwennol, which is Welsh for swallow, but you all knew that anyway. There was a certain amount of trouble at t'mill over the business of Welsh nomenclature, but I think that it makes a change from boring old Ranter and Ruby. Gwennol's dam is called Gwyddfid (I think), which is Welsh for honeysuckle, but you all knew that anyway; I think we might have one of those next year.

Hounds' names are very traditional and many of the names suggested by Peter Beckford are in current use. Some have fallen into desuetude, however. I cannot ever remember coming across a Cherriper, or a Climbank. If you can persuade your Hunt Treasurer to walk a puppy, why not let him have a Fleece'm; and please can someone tell me what are, respectively, a Larum, and a Palafox?

I do not think that I have ever been hunting with a Harlot either.

I am always fascinated by the way the Americans improve, and brighten, the English language. I have quite a lot of Americanisms that I use regularly, mostly gleaned from watching the films of Mr Clint Eastwood, of whom I am a devoted fan. My favourite one of the moment is the description of someone who is a bit weak in the head as 'not being very well wrapped'. I could not have put it better myself. What I think could be improved on is American officialese: things like 'fuel-wise, we are in a totally negative situation' when what you mean is that the coal scuttle is empty. However, I suppose that 'stomach awareness' must be better than feeling sick, and I never fail to ask my son if he has performed his 'bowel duty'.

There has been quite a lot of post recently. There was a long, and very interesting letter from a man in Leicestershire, discussing various hunting points. On the whole I agreed with him, but on one basic point we differed: he suggested that it was not necessary for hounds to catch foxes for them to show good sport. I could not disagree more strongly. The difference between a well-blooded pack of hounds and their opposites is as different as strong whisky and flat Coca-Cola. It is all the difference between following on the 'line' of a fox, and hunting the fox with dash, drive and determination. Then you will get good sport, and good hunting.

Some people who hunt think less about catching the fox than those who do not. Anyone who has hacked home with hounds will know that the almost invariable question from those you meet is, 'How many did you catch?' Should the

huntsman have to answer that the day has produced a negative vulpine termination situation, he may well be subjected to strident criticism, and cries of, 'What a load of inorganic disposal matter.'

A canny friend of mine has found a way of avoiding this problem without lying through his gritted teeth, like some huntsmen do. When asked the fateful question, after a fruitless day, he replies, 'No more than one,' which is truthful, correct and totally misleading; in fact a perfect parliamentary answer.

I suppose that most MsFH get their share of anonymous letters. I have all my choicer examples on file, except for one that I returned. Most anonymous letters run to six pages of emotional incoherence, but this one was admirably succinct. It said: 'Up yours Fatso.'

Now it just so happened that I knew who the writer was, for reasons that I will not bore you with. The letter seemed to me to be quite specific as to what the writer required me to do with it, so at the first appropriate moment I did. Then I sent it back, first class post, but unsigned. It is the only anonymous letter that I have ever written – if that is the right word.

I am having trouble with the Vice-Chairman. He was telling an appreciative audience in the Mart canteen that the Committee had put me in for a free transfer, but could not find anybody to take me. Rearing up like a piece of fried bread, I pointed out that I had not moved 120 miles to be insulted, when at least I could be insulted in comfort where I was. That might be true, said the VC, but at least I was being insulted in a different language. That is a very good point, but the trouble is that I am beginning to understand it.

At the magnates luncheon, the Colonel was holding forth on the caravan that he had recently bought, and what a great blessing it was for improved mobility. A lesser magnate said that were they not beastly things to drive? Absolutely no problem, said the Colonel, he always sent it on with a man, and drove down afterwards. The magnates thought about this, and an objection was raised. Not all of them, it was pointed out, had men; absolutely no problem, said the Colonel, you have all got wives.

I told Mrs James this story, and she said that it was much too near the truth to be remotely amusing. It indicated, she said, the typical feudalistic, chauvinistic approach of the average, northern male who regards Woman as a mere drudge, and plaything, and what was more, now that I had mentioned the subject there were one or two other matters that she would like to bring to my attention. Did I not realize . . . but by this time I was through the door, and travelling well in the direction of the tall timber. I must remember to leave my misplaced attempts at humour at the back door, alongside my rubber boots.

I was thinking the other night how fortunate I have been in the men who have worked with me in hunting. As a young man I was fortunate enough to work with hunt servants of the old school, men who had been through the 'mill' and survived. For these men perfection was only just good enough; there could be no skimping, no short cuts, and you did the job until it was done right.

They were the product of hard and almost brutal training when they were young men. If you could not stick it, then you got out of hunt service. I remember an old huntsman telling me that his first job in scarlet was as third whipper-in to the Essex Staghounds. There was some form of van for the hounds, but one Saturday evening he and the second horseman were left in the dimpsey with five horses to hack home, and home was forty-five miles away. They got the horses home at 0330 hours. The next morning our young man got into the kennels at 0603, instead of 0600, and was given notice. He was reprieved but was told that if he could not do the job properly in future, then he had better go.

He survived and became a famous huntsman, but he learnt the hard way. He told me another story too. He was whipping-in to his uncle, who was probably the most famous professional of his day, but who ate whippers-in for breakfast. Our hero wanted to get married, and went to ask permission of the great man, as was the custom. The great man gave permission, and said that he supposed that a honeymoon would be required. Well that would be in order; the marriage was to happen on a Friday, and the nephew need not be back in the kennel until 0600 on the Sunday, and on no account was he to be late.

I am not suggesting that this sort of treatment was necessary to the making of great hunt servants, but it did mean that only the fittest survived, and that the men who had been through the mill were trained men, and able to train others.

The thing that saddens me is that while hunt service continues to attract young men of exceptional character, the number of establishments that are capable of training these young men properly become fewer all the time. This is partly due to economics. There are fewer opportunities for young men to work their way through the old pipeline of the kennels and the stables and thus gain a solid grounding in all aspects of their craft. The old chain of strapper, second horseman, second whipper-in, first whipper-in, has almost ceased to exist.

What happens now is that able young men are promoted too quickly; men are now becoming huntsmen, and kennel-huntsmen, at an age and a stage of experience when they should be looking for their first post as first whipper-in to an experienced huntsman. This situation is not their fault, but it does mean that a lot of men with great potential fail through lack of experience, and a lot of those who survive are only half-trained.

Half-trained men are unlikely to produce the men they train to any higher standard, and thus the spiral tends to be downwards. Whilst I had my *Baily's* out, I went through it and totted up the kennels that I reckoned to be capable of producing a well-trained man. There are over 200 packs of foxhounds in England, Wales and Scotland, but the number of kennels that I marked I could have added up on ten fingers and ten toes. Food for thought?

It is my custom after breakfast to smoke a pipe on the thunderbox. I regard both operations as essential to my mental and physical well-being. Dogs may whine, children scream, wives tantrum, and sheriffs batter on the door. It matters not, for a few precious minutes, with the pipe drawing nicely, I am alone with my thoughts.

When I was thus enthroned the other morning, it occurred to me that nowhere in the sporting press have I ever seen an in-depth study of the MFH. So what better subject to consider at the start of the hunting season? Come with me now and let us see if we can throw any light on the habits and psychology of this shy, elusive little creature.

Perhaps the first question that we should ask is why on earth anybody should want to become an MFH?

After many years study of the genus I have come to the conclusion that MsFH may be divided into four main categories: the Dedicated, the Inherited, the Achieved, and the Damn-it-all-Bertie-someone's-got-to-do-it. I think that we will take them in reverse order, for no very good reason except that that is how I feel. Right? Right.

Most hunts have a sticky passage at some stage of their existence. A Mastership ends, no successor appears and the committee takes control. The one thing that has united the committee all these years has been the conviction that they have been providing the Mastership with far too much money, most of which has gone down the magisterial throat in liquid form.

Now, at long last, they can rationalize the expenditure and run the hunt properly. Oh Unhappy Band of Pilgrims! Before the end of the first season, lifelong friendships have gone into voluntary liquidation, the Chief Constable has his Special Patrol

Group standing by at hunt committee meetings, and everybody is going to have to dig deep into their pockets. A Master must be found, but who? And where from? The argument rages long and loud, and then someone has a brainwave.

Over in the corner sits dear old Major Luce-Rayne. He is fat, stone deaf, and has slept through every committee meeting for the last ten years. Never will he sleep through another. Poor man, he wakes with a start to find a circle of faces leering at him. The Chairman is haranguing him on duty, saving the ship, all hands to the pump, etc, etc.

'What? What?' cries the poor old booby.

'You've just been elected Master,' bellows the Chairman.

'But I don't want to be Master.'

'Damn it all, Bertie' says the Chairman, 'someone's got to do it.' And do it he does, just long enough to unite the committee in condemnation of his regime, and for him to worry himself into a nice little coronary.

The Achieved MFH is a totally different creature. He wants to be a MFH. It is probable that he is a man who has done well in life, and has taken to foxhunting because he reckons he meets a better class of people out hunting than he does at the golf club. Who could disagree with him?

Foxhunting opens up a whole new world to him, and on top of this world is the MFH. Our man is used to power: he is used to manipulating boards; underlings quake when summoned to the Presence; he has stripped more assets than you have had mugs of Ovaltine; and yet, and yet . . .

Out hunting he is amazed by this red-coated megalomaniac who constantly exhorts his followers to: '— their — up their —' and whose exhortations are received in respectful silence. In the course of the evening *après chasse,* he sees that this same man is apparently allowed to get drunk, molest wives and do incredibly interesting, and impertinent, things to Duchesses, without let or hindrance.

This, he decides, is where it is really at. He wants a slice of the action, and why not?

It is heartening to note that not a few Achieved MsFH

achieve great success as foxhunters. However, I suspect that a lot more resign their Masterships, sadder, wiser and quite a bit poorer. Let them console themselves with the thought that during their term of office they will have made a major contribution to foxhunting (their Joint-Masters will have seen to that). There is that splendid equestrian portrait for the board-room wall, and the Duchess was too, too exquisitely grateful for all his efforts.

You might think that it is a lovesome thing to Inherit a pack of foxhounds. You would be right too, always provided that (a) you want a pack of foxhounds, and (b) that your ancestors have left enough gilt in the piggybank to provide for their upkeep. Just think how tiresome it would be to have forty couple of hounds land, with a thump, on your doorstep, when all you want to do is to broke stocks in a sanitized City office, or retire to Antibes and write a treatise on the demise of the Steam Tram.

The unkindest cut of all is to inherit the family pack to which you are devoted, with a deep and earnest devotion, and then, on opening the family coffer to pay the wages you find that it contains a 1978 Cheltenham Spring Meeting race card, a half-empty bottle of Gee's Linctus, a blurred photograph of your father carving a round off an unknown lady, and £5.36 in coin of the realm.

So all good fortune to those who inherit their hounds. May they also inherit the skill, the will, and the wherewithal.

At last we come to the Dedicated Master. We have to have him. Foxhunting would not function without him. But let us face facts, he does tend to be a bit of a pain in the rear echelons, and is often smelly as well.

Dedicated Masters usually catch the disease during their formative years and, unlike measles and acne, it tends to stay with them for life. It is a distressing complaint, especially for those who are forced into close contact with the patient. The patient becomes incapable of normal speech and converses solely in grunts, passages from Beckford, and the more lyrical part of the Foxhound Kennel Stud Book. When under the influence of alcohol (often) the patient tends to make hunting noises.

There will be a marked physical deterioration. The face will become empurpled, and the patient will emit a strange effluvium, that is a mixture of dead sheep, old hounds and green oils. A side effect of the condition is a tendency to collect and discard wives (usually other people's) at an alarming rate. However, this is a passing phase as the patient eventually has so many terriers in his house that there is no room for a wife anyway.

So there we are. I hope that this article will give you food for thought. Whatever category you may think it proper to include your MFH in, just pause before you stick another pin in his effigy and ask yourself:

'Could I do better?'

Addresses always fascinate me. I once lived in a part of the country that abounded in Halls and Granges; the let down was that, when you actually got to some of them, they were two up and two down with an outside khazi. On the other hand, something called 'The Cottage' tended to have ten bedrooms, six bathrooms and an indoor swimming pool. A couple of years ago I had to go to Ulster, and I was intrigued to discover that every house there has a street number, regardless of where, or what it is. Thus No. 1 Mulligatawny Road might well be a three-bedroomed bungalow, while No. 2 is a gothic mansion standing in its own 12,000 acres. I am not quite clear what the significance of this idea is, but I have probably contravened the Official Secrets Act by even mentioning the matter. So it will be me for the slammer, with the Editor looking pale, but noble, as he protests to the High Court about the Freedom of the Press.

I have often laughed about gout. It conjures up images of a heavy hand on the port decanter and an ex-Indian colonel, with a heavily-bandaged foot, being pushed along the front at Eastbourne, in a bath chair, and a rotten temper. Now I know why the colonel was in a bad temper: gout is quite exquisitely painful. However, I have found a cure. There is some marvellous stuff called 'Fiery Jack', which is, in effect, a red blister for humans, and is quite the finest thing for strains and aches.

An eminent sporting journalist arrived on my doorstep recently, complete with a badly-strained riding muscle. We rubbed his thigh with Fiery Jack; that is to say, we gave him some Fiery Jack to rub on his thigh (we do not want any misunderstandings in a family publication, do we?). He passed a completely sleepless night, but his riding muscle was cured. I rubbed some Fiery Jack on the gout-affected joint, and spent a day hobbling about in appalling agony, but by evening the gout had gone, bludgeoned into submission, I suspect.

This is a cautionary tale. Once upon a time there was a certain Pony Club camp. To entertain the children in the evenings, it was decided to hire a video machine and show films of an entertaining and educational nature. A harassed Pony Club mum (and, in my experience, no other kind exists) was deputed to organize the whole thing. At last, when all the little dears were settled down in front of the box, the keepers retired to kick their shoes off, wiggle their toes and do whatever off-duty keepers do. Peace reigned.

At last a keeper decided to have a peek and see how the little ones were getting on. The Little Ones were watching the screen, totally enthralled by all the naked ladies and gentlemen doing strange things to each other. It all looked such fun, and they were quite upset when the keeper hit the emergency stop button, and had hysterics. At the subsequent drumhead court martial, the harassed mum said that the label was in Swedish but she had understood the nice man to say that it was something to do with Snow White and the Seven Dwarfs; and so it was, after a fashion.

I do not like hunting on Christmas Eve. If you hunt Christmas Eve and Boxing Day, in most years it means that the staff get a pretty thin Christmas Day, and I do not see why they should not make as much of the holiday as they can. It is no use your telling me that Christmas Eve is a holiday meet and nice for the kiddies: you and your repulsive kiddies all absent yourselves from your places of work and education for at least a fortnight over Christmas and the New Year, thus having plenty of time to go hunting. You do not need Christmas Eve.

I used to dread Christmas and, to be honest, I still regard it with a certain amount of suspicion. For a long time, Christmas was ruined for me by Boxing Day; I used to dread the Boxing Day meet. It was very important to me, when I was a bachelor, that I spent Christmas with my parents.

If I was weak enough to allow myself to be bullied into hunting on Christmas Eve, and I am an immensely malleable person, I was faced with a 100-mile drive after hunting to spend a few hours in front of the family yule log. After lunch on Christmas Day, when all I yearned to do, apart from loosening several trouser buttons, was to sink into a hoggish coma, I was faced with the 100 miles in reverse, and Christmas night with a cold drumstick to keep me company.

I wonder if you know anything about turkeys, apart from how to eat them. I kept turkeys once. To be exact I looked after them for a large agri-business that specialized in turkeys. I rented one of my sheds to them, and also undertook to feed, water and bed them down. The actual work only took about an hour a day and was not terribly arduous, especially as I usually allowed Mrs James to do it. It is very important that one's family should feel involved, I always think.

In fact it was the best paying enterprise that I have ever undertaken; when I say that it paid even better than writing for *Shooting Times,* then you will understand what I mean. The

only trouble was the turkeys themselves. Turkeys are stupid, neurotic and thoroughly unattractive birds, especially in bulk, and above all they are noisy. The only time a turkey is quiet is when it is on the point of expiring, which seemed to happen pretty regularly. However, they did us very well for a time, and I still look forward to eating them.

Boxing Day is the only day in the season on which I would rather do almost anything than hunt. It is usually a shambles.

One year there was the Great Boxing Day Riot. We had had a fairly typical morning, hunting from road-block to road-block. As the hunting got more and more local, more and more people left their cars and took to their feet. By the time the fox took to the local scrapyard, there must have been some two hundred people milling about. Somehow the fox broke from the scrapyard into an adjacent covert with the hounds tight at him. The crowd broke too. With an almighty yell, the whole lot piled into the covert with the hounds. I saw one man waving an umbrella, and another one a sheath knife.

Hounds caught the fox in the covert, amid scenes of great jubilation. Now, you will say that this was a disgraceful way for hunt supporters to behave, and I would agree with you. The rub was that these were not hunt supporters, within the meaning of the act. The great majority of them were total strangers to me. They were just members of the great British public, who are totally opposed to hunting, as we never cease to be told.

After Christmas comes the New Year. I have never been able to get very excited about the New Year, but people in the north do tend to get excited about it. In fact some of them tend to get very excited about it indeed. The spirit moves them in some very mysterious ways: some try to climb down the front of their neighbours' wives' dresses; some dance, some sing, and some just lie down and blow bubbles in such a position that you are bound to fall over them when trying to find your coat.

I have no doubt that similar things happen in Pinner, or Purley (well no, perhaps not in Purley) but what makes it different in the north is the sheer stamina of the participants who seem to be able to keep up the relentless pressure for days, and nights, on end. I envy their fortitude but I have more sense than to try to keep up with them. Besides, it takes me two weeks to recover from the two glasses of Bristol Cream that I allow myself on Christmas morning.

With the New Year are supposed to come resolutions. In the gloom induced by post-festivity-triste, one is inclined to resolve to do, or not to do, some fairly unlikely things. I have long since given up any attempts to improve myself: after all, it is a pretty good waste of time trying to improve perfection. There is a much more interesting time to be had out of improving other people.

Dogs have a great homing instinct, or some do. We have all heard stories of the way hounds sent to distant kennels have made their way home over great distances. Yet some do not seem to be able to find their way home five miles. What interests me is the way some dogs sense where they are in a car. I have a terrier at the moment which always knows when we get to a mile or so from home.

The best example of this instinct that I can remember was when I took an old foxhound bitch from Badminton back home to the Puckeridge. She settled down at once in the car, and slept until we got within about three miles of Brent Pelham when she suddenly woke up and became very eager and excited. She knew that she was nearly home, but how did she know?

A certain famous foxhunter did not like people wasting his time. If anybody wanted to look at his hounds, they had to pass a test. The first hound to be pulled out for inspection would be one of quite extraordinary ugliness. The majority of people would feel constrained to say something nice about it out of politeness; whereupon the great man would say: 'Well, you obviously know nothing about hounds, so let us go and look at the horses instead.' I have never dared try that one – and anyway I do not have any ugly hounds.

Someone asked me why a fox is called 'Charley'. I have always understood that it came from Mr Charles James Fox who was an eminent Whig politician in the early nineteenth century. He was by all accounts a sharp and clever man. I think that he was responsible for what I have always thought to be one of the best retorts ever. He had been goading Lord Newcastle, who may have been Prime Minister at the time (I may say that I am dredging all this up through thirty years of memory sludge); and the noble lord rounded on Mr Fox and cried that he would 'infallibly either be hanged or die of the pox'. Without hesitation Fox replied that 'that would depend on whether he embraced the noble lord's principles, or his mistresses'. How I wish I could think of answers like that. I notice an increasing tendency to refer to foxes as 'Basil', after Basil Brush. I am second to none in my admiration for Mr Brush, but I bet that he could not answer like old Charles James could.

Another old name for a fox was Dan Russel, but I have never been able to discover the origin of that one. Someone told me that it was Saxon, but it does not sound very Saxon; it would be Leofric, or Ethelbert, not to mention Athelstane. Perhaps someone could shed some light.

How are you on the bagpipes? I rather like the sound myself although I must say that for enclosed entertainment

I prefer the Northumbrian pipes to the larger Scottish variety. The Northumbrian pipes have the added advantage of being worked by an elbow-driven set of bellows thus allowing the player to sing as well, although this is not always an unmixed blessing. I like the names of the tunes too: 'The 83rd's farewell to Union Street, Plymouth', or 'Captain Murdoch Macdougall's Lament', perhaps as a result of dallying too much in Union Street. I have a sneaky hope that someone might feel inspired to write the 'Arthur James Rant' one day.

However, not everyone shares my taste for the pipes. I think particularly of a naval man I met once who at one time lived in a married quarter in Greenock. The quarter was half of a semi. The other half was occupied by the MacBlank of MacBlank, who had come down in the world a bit, but was by no means out. Although the old gentleman was reduced to a Greenock semi, he was still ceremoniously piped into dinner every night. The naval man found that a thin mutual wall did little to diminish the decibel level. I am afraid that there goes one man who will never be a convert to the pipes.

Now that we have started on the subject of elderly gentlemen let us consider the plight of one such who found himself in considerable difficulty when the last of his aged retainers fell off her perch, leaving him with only a 'weekly' to minister to his needs. The problem was that the Elderly Gentleman had never made a bed in his life, and was damned if he was going to start at his age. He resolved the problem very neatly. There was a large number of bedrooms in the house, and every Friday the weekly lady made up seven beds in seven bedrooms, thus providing the Elderly Gentleman with a week's supply of beds to sleep in.

Yet another Elderly Gentleman whom I met twenty years ago, and who has now handed in his dinner pail, was a great hunting man all his life. As a young man he had worked in the City, and used to hunt with the Surrey Staghounds. He could remember running across the 'Putney Vale', which he described as 'a bit market gardeney'. However, I suppose that is a better memory of Putney than mine which is of a place I only went to because I fell asleep on a District Line train and woke up there. I would not fancy hunting the Putney Vale nowadays.

I am gradually returning to normal health. I have just emerged from a coma induced by a 'Herds' Supper'. Herds' Suppers are an interesting feature of life in the Borders. Each area holds its own and they are more correctly known as 'Shepherds' and Farmworkers' Suppers'. You start the evening at 7.30 with a supper which is, necessarily, solid and sustaining. At 8.30 the Chairman pounds the table with the sort of fist that commands respect and attention, for the loyal toast. Then follows some four hours of speeches and entertainment. There are normally toasts, and replies, to Agriculture, the Hunt (which is how I weasel my way in), Shepherds and Farmworkers. Between each speech there is entertainment of some sort, either musical or a story-teller.

Now the only way you can get people to sit through four hours of that sort of thing is by lubricating them liberally and having speakers and entertainers of a very high order, all of which happens. The entertainers are nearly all from the Agricultural and Allied Trades, and all I can say is that you will hear nothing better on the telly.

Little Jim came up from Yorkshire to do the Hunt toast, and he said next morning that he could not remember when he had laughed so much: at least I think that is what he said, it is sometimes difficult to hear what people are saying when they have their head buried in their hands. It is just possible that Little Jim may have had the smallest touch of a headache, because whilst the formal part of the supper is over by midnight, it would be dishonest of me to lead you to suppose that everyone then collects their hats and coats and makes for home and the bedtime mug of Ovaltine. Things continued apace until the Bar announced that he had run out of whisky, which is a pretty dramatic announcement for a Northumbrian Bar to make. This did break things up a bit, but it was not long before a strong team were settled round the accordion at Tom's place, where the whisky had not run out.

I eventually got Little Jim away and then found a deputation camped on my doorstep in urgent need of a medicinal dram. All in all it was 0400 when I crept into bed with the prospect of a full two and a half hours sleep before me before feeding the sheep and going hunting. We did not have a very good day's hunting; there was a suggestion that the Master and huntsman was somewhat off colour; I wonder why?

My pick-up has just been undersealed against the ravages of the winter weather. It is a hard-working machine what with towing trailers and shepherding, and it does tend to get a bit untidy. However, I did take exception to what the work-shop foreman said when I collected the machine. He said that it was the first time that he had ever had to put covers on the seats to keep the mechanic clean. Well I mean, I think that that is a bit thick, what?

On the subject of vehicles I always have a firm intention of buying British, but the sad fact is that the British motor industry refuses to cater for my needs. In particular it refuses to make a car that is wide enough for me to sit in without my right shoulder being jammed against the door, or high enough for me to be able to wear a hat without flattening it on the roof. To be absolutely fair, I can fit well in a Range Rover, but I am unable to fit it into my budget. I expect that I would fit in a Roller, but that is out for the reason heretofore expressed and also it would not be terribly practical – although I believe that Australian graziers, who have them, find the glass panel behind the driver very useful when they have a few sheep in the back. So having excluded the two Rs there is not a single suitable British vehicle that I have been able to discover and I think that this is very sad.

Be that as it may, I have a Swedish car and a Japanese pick-up, both of which supply ample seat room for the ample seat, and plenty of room for the elbow and shoulder. May I suggest to the British Motor Industry that they consider what the Japs and Swedes have already found out: people are larger than they used to be (very definitely in my case). I would like to be patriotic but I do not see why I should not be comfortable as well.

I am looking for a horse and if the usual channels fail me I may have to follow the example of the cavalry officer in Germany. He was enjoying an evening's cultural entertainment at a club on the Reeperbahn, which is the centre of cultural life in Hamburg (or so I understand). Part of the entertainment was provided by a lady and a horse, although I think it unlikely that you will ever see this particular combination at the Horse of the Year show.

'That's a damned good sort,' said the officer, and none of his fascinated companions disagreed. On the completion of the act, our hero summoned the manager and in pidgin German asked him to name a price. It took some time for everyone to understand that far from wishing to improve his *Kultur* with the young lady, he wanted to buy her horse. He did, and I understand that it made a very good polo pony. It is an interesting idea, but I think that I am going to have some difficulty convincing Mrs James that I am only going to Hamburg to look for horses.

I lived for a time on the Wiltshire Downs and found them fascinating. I should love to have seen them before they were all ploughed. My then Hunt Chairman, who had farmed and hunted there all his life, remembered the old open downs, when a man could ride for many miles on old turf, and never meet a fence. There was precious little old turf left by the time I got there but it was still a most interesting part of the world.

One of its best features was the network of old drove roads that criss-crossed the downs; you could ride, or walk, for miles on these old chalk roads, and see not a living soul. These are the green roads of England, the old roads that have been used ever since man started travelling from one place to another, which must appeal to anyone with a little imagination.

I have just been reading one of W. H. Hudson's books, in which he laments the rape of the downs by the Army (1902). I wonder what the old boy would think about it if he came back today. The Larkhill and Imber ranges are the only stretches of virgin downland left, and nature has adapted in her usual way. Animal, bird and plant life thrives amongst the slit trenches and shell craters in a way that is impossible on the great prairies of barley.

Twenty years ago I visited the village of Imber. It was rather battered, as the houses were used for instruction in street fighting, and the church was surrounded by a zariba of barbed wire. But if you stood there on a quiet spring day, with the larks singing on the downs, you could picture a downland village as it must have been fifty years ago. Then the Army started mortaring me, and I made a tactical withdrawal to shorten my lines of communication.

At the time of writing, my ewes are running on one side of a small valley. The other side of the valley is into winter corn and for the last month it has supported a large gaggle of Brent geese who seem very settled. Some years ago I was in Pennsylvania, USA. It was Easter Sunday morning and I woke up suddenly thinking that I could hear hounds running, but it was not, it was geese. Geese flying north: thousands, tens of thousands of them, it took the main body over half an hour to pass; it was a sight and sound that I have never forgotten.

It is a nasty shock to the system to have one's cherished beliefs shattered. I am getting quite an old and smelly fox-hunter now, and it had never occurred to me that there was any way of going foxhunting apart from the way that I did it. I had always assumed that the correct way was to leave the meet punctually and reasonably sober and then to pursue, and hopefully catch, as many foxes as possible until darkness or lack of horse power foreclosed on the day's work. This does not include the hours of freezing darkness spent upside down in a hole listening for the terrier that they were nearly up to four hours ago.

But this, my children, is not the way of culture and sophistication. My way is that of the untutored barbarian. I realized the error of my ways whilst listening to a friend of mine who was sent to revive the flagging fortunes of a fashionable pack of foxhounds. This is what you do.

You move off at 1100 hours; at 1300 hours you arrive at a pre-arranged spot for luncheon. You do this even if it means stopping hounds and hacking four miles to the trysting place. Luncheon lasts from 1300–1400 hours. At 1500 you go home.

To be fair, luncheon is referred to as 'second horses', the second horses being sent each day to the same pre-arranged spot. In the hour that changing from one horse to another apparently requires, the fashionable foxhunter refortifies the inner man who tends to be weakened after a full two hours in, and around, the saddle. Then he is hoisted on to his second horse, full of vim and vigour that see him through the hour's hunting that will fill the gap before the traditional hunting tea.

I wish to make a full and frank confession. In the days when I had second horses, it was not like that. The second horse would appear, in a puff of smoke, and would come neatly alongside to starboard: horn from one case to the other; Roger off to starboard and both horses by their heads; a nimble (?!?) vault from one saddle to the other; feet into previously adjusted stirrups; cast off forrard; full ahead both engines: total time, approximately 30 seconds.

It saddens me to say it, but my friend is an uncultured boor like me, and I do hope that he will not foist his uncouth ways on fashionable foxiana. But if the Stock Market does appear to be a bit jittery, do not get too worried; it is simply a lot of hunting stockbrokers with indigestion.

I was properly rebuked the other day for turning up at a hunt wine-and-cheese party looking about as cheerful as

Crewe Station on a wet Sunday afternoon. I had had a very bad day's hunting; and I wanted all the world to share my suffering. I do not like going out after hunting. It takes me the whole evening to wind down and all I want to do is to have a long, hot bath and collapse in my armchair to savour my triumphs or lick my wounds as the case may be. I was trying to explain this to Joe but he said that he thought I was talking nonsense; when he was hunting, he had gone out for a drink every night after hunting, and he had helped a bit with the whipping-in. Bless his heart, that is rather like saying to a surgeon that you, too, can put on a piece of sticking plaster. It is an old and true saying that: 'None but a huntsman knows a huntsman's cares.' Hunting hounds is a mental strain and I venture to say that any huntsman who is not shattered at the end of the day has not been giving his all to the job.

It is a job, too, however much you may love it, and requires total concentration and mental commitment. This is why huntsmen sometimes get a little short-tempered. But it is no use expecting anyone to understand fully unless they have tried the job themselves. Just try to remember that whilst you go hunting for pleasure and relaxation, the poor beggar with the trumpet is flogging his guts out to provide that pleasure. So, go on, give him a sniff of your flask.

I telephoned a friend of mine, in the south, the other day: 'How is Muggins getting on?' I asked.

'He will never make a huntsman as long as he has a hole in his face,' came the reply. 'No venom.'

It is a fact that hounds take their cue from their huntsman and if the huntsman lacks the killer instinct, then the hounds too are likely to lack that edge. The huntsman must *want* to catch the fox his hounds are hunting more than anything else in the world at that moment. I heard of a man who turned down the chance to hunt a well-known pack of hounds on two days of the week because he felt that he lacked the killer instinct; and I think that he did absolutely the right thing.

We were discussing another huntsman who has some reputation as a foxcatcher and my friend said: 'You can see him when he goes to draw; he is grinding his teeth and going, "Gnash, gnash; fox, fox", and his hounds are grinding their teeth and going "Gnash, gnash; fox, fox".' In fact, when you think about it, that would not be a bad slogan for every huntsman to have pegged to the wall above his shaving mirror and to say to himself every morning.

It must be very difficult having your kennels, or your farm come to that, on the side of a busy road. If you drive up and down the A1, you can see many substantial steadings bang beside the main road. In the days of horse-drawn vehicles it must have been interesting, and useful, to live right on the Great North Road; now it must be a nightmare. Although I suspect that most of the farms I have in mind have nothing livelier than a sugarbeet on them and they are not likely to gallop through a gate and cause havoc on the northbound carriageway, to have livestock, and more especially a kennel, beside a busy road, doesn't bear thinking about.

Once upon a time there was a certain foxhound kennels beside which ran a road. This road was not actually that busy but there was a certain punter who lived in the neighbouring village and who drove to work past the kennels. This punter was always late, whether it was because of the nubile charms of the wife of his bosom, or a more intellectual wrestle with

The Times crossword, I know not. The fact was that whatever the reason, he was always late for work and used to go past the kennels like the proverbial dose of salts.

There were some very nasty moments and the huntsman approached the punter on several occasions, and begged him to mend his ways. I regret to say that all appeals were of no avail and the punter continued to Jehu. But the huntsman was a downy bird and he took unto himself a plastic tillage bag; this bag he left lying in the road. The first morning the punter came speeding by and drove over the tillage bag. The second morning the punter came speeding by and drove over the tillage bag. On the third morning the huntsman put a concrete block in the tillage bag . . . !

I was leafing idly through the MFHA directory of hunts the other day, and I realized that I hardly knew any of the rising generation of hunt servants. Fifteen years ago I could have put a face to most of the huntsmen, and kennel huntsmen, in the book, and would have known a good number of them. Now the majority of the men I knew seem to have disappeared from the scene, through age, vice or unsoundness, as we all shall in time.

It is sad to think that some able men have gone out of hunt service before their time, leaving hunting a little poorer for their passing. Others have gone at the end of long careers, having been giants in their time. Others have been forced to retire prematurely, through injury, or ill health; hunting is still a very demanding life physically; modern technology has not had a great impact on kennel work but perhaps, even now, someone is inventing a microcomputer that will skin and cut up a sheep.

Mrs James pointed out to me that ever since I have had Joint-Masters, at least one of them has been female. She is quite right, having been one of the elect herself at one time. All the ladies who have been joint with me have all had one thing in common: apart from their personal charm, they have all absolutely terrified me. It is this fact to which I attribute my survival as a foxhunter of pretty limited talent. I was saved from the debacle of my first season as an MFH by two ladies of quite stunning authority who hauled me whimpering from the wreckage, dusted me down, kicked my bum and, thereafter, kept me firmly pointed in the direction of restitude. I owe them both a great debt of gratitude.

The basic training provided by these two ladies has meant that, ever since, I have been as putty in the hands of my female Joint-Masters, and between them and Mrs James I have become pretty well moulded over the years, until I am probably the best-schooled Master/huntsman in the business; I never dribble port down my shirt front, I always eat all my rice pudding, and I always have the horses home by half past three, well, nearly always. There was an awful evening (still known as 'Black Tuesday') when I did not get the horses home until 10.15pm for reasons that I will not bore you with, but which might have been connected with certain protracted excavations, but that was a solitary lapse in an otherwise spotless career. I understand that my next application for parole has a limited chance of success.

I am worried about my Hunt Chairman; he was looking a bit out of sorts the other day, so I tried to cheer him up by telling him that two of my previous Hunt Chairmen had, at various times, suffered from cardiac problems and had stopped being Hunt Chairmen. The Chairman looked very thoughtful and said that he thought that he could understand their problem; I cannot think what he meant.

What of the sport? you ask. Well, if you insist, I suppose I shall have to talk about it. December was not a bad month, overall, although perhaps a rather better month for the hounds than the ladies and gentlemen. We did have one outstanding day and, by that, I mean that I rate it as one of the ten best hound hunts that I have known.

The meet was not a popular one, being on the edge of the forestry, and the field was very select. Hounds killed the first fox fairly smartly, and as they were breaking it up we heard a single hound speaking on the hill above. It was a brilliant sunny day, with lots of gossamer webs; scent seemed poor. Hounds niggled the line on and, as they got tuned in, the pace improved. It would mean nothing to you if I told you the names of all the places we went to. There were two things that made the day remarkable. The first was the scent; hounds went the same pace with the fox fifteen minutes gone as they did when we bolted him from a road drain during the hunt; they were never able to change up a gear.

The other remarkable thing was that the hunt took place almost entirely in bye, with just two short excursions onto the hill, and back down again. Hounds hunted remorselessly over winter corn, rape, through stock foil of every description. They were touched only twice, on the two occasions that the fox ran a road. How I longed for them to catch that fox, but darkness saved him, and when I say darkness, the cars had their headlights on when I finally picked them up. It really was a pretty hound hunt. How far? Twenty-two miles as hounds ran, with a 6-mile point!

I am second to nobody in my admiration for the Country Landowners' Association; as sound a body of citizens as exists. The only thing I have against them is that I understand they are responsible for producing a particular type of gate latch that is not only totally impossible to open from a horse, but is almost impossible to open on your feet, without the loss of half a thumb.

In the past, the CLA got some stick for being somewhat equivocal in its public pronouncements on hunting. There were even those malign people who suggested that the membership consisted entirely of vulpicides and suburban garden owners. I will not hear such talk about such a splendid body of men. The reason why the CLA sat on the fence over hunting is that none of them could get their blasted gates open.

The field were sitting comfortably on the hill, watching the huntsman, in a hurry (and a temper), struggling with a succession of somewhat decrepit and well-wired gates. The field watched the proceedings with a detached interest, realizing that their isolation precluded any help that they might have been inclined to give. They even wagered, in a mild way, as to when flash point might be reached. When it was, they listened appreciatively to the explosion.

'Most interesting,' said a farmer. 'My gates are made by Gush and Dent. Jim's seem to be made by a firm called F—— it.'

My son considers it something of a mixed blessing having a huntsman for a father, but he has got off more lightly than some. There was a certain man, some years ago, who was forced to come out of hunt service through ill health. He had rather weak insides which he attributed to the fact that his father had always given his children a wormball whenever he wormed the hounds.

Another old huntsman, attending the nursing home where his wife had been 'brought to bed' was upset to find that she had only had a 'bitch whelp' and offered the sister five bob to put her down; it was always a matter of some surprise to him that his generous offer was refused. However, he became very fond of the child and christened her Faithful after his favourite brood bitch.

I do not suppose you have ever given the matter much thought, but one of the problems that sometimes confronts a huntsman is answering the call of nature, him being, as you might say, in the public eye. This is one reason why you should not follow huntsmen about the coverts; if you do and you see something you do not like, then it is your fault, not his. Still, as my mother always says, you will not see anything that God did not make.

There was a certain famous huntsman who always used his hunting horn as an aid to relief. When quizzed by his son as to the reason for this, he replied: 'Urine hardens the lips, my boy.' Personally, I am prepared to take his word for it.

I have been guilty of hubris, and am justly suffering. There have been some very nasty cold and influenza bugs flying about up here. I lost no chance and told any sufferer I could trap that I had never had a cold since coming to Northumberland, which was true. But even then fate was filling the sock with wet sand. I had to go down to London, and left a bright, sunny Newcastle to arrive in a London wrapped in freezing fog.

I am not surprised that this country has a balance of payments crisis: the cost of heating every shop and office, up to the 95°F that Londoners apparently require, must be enormous. Why not have a maximum indoor temperature of 60°F which must be hot enough for anybody and, if it is not, let them buy sweaters, thereby greatly benefiting the domestic knitting industry, and also my wool cheque.

I staggered back to Heathrow limp and sweating, and watched with horrified fascination people wearing fur coats and the sort of coats that would have been useful on the top of Snowdon in January, but seemed out of place in an atmosphere that a crude antipodean friend of mine would have described as being like a 'stockman's jockstrap'. Anyway, the upshot of the whole grisly episode was that I came down the next morning with as nasty a touch of London Lurgy as I can remember.

An interesting, if rather grisly, item. One of our followers was having trouble. If one of his ewes got on its back, something was coming along and chewing bits out of her. This is not recommended procedure and was causing not a little unhappiness, not least to the sheep concerned. At first, foxes were blamed but somehow it did not sound fox-like and the strange thing was that these attacks only happened in fields close to a river. As you will have rightly guessed, the culprits were mink who have fairly recently found their way into this area. They have not chosen a very good way to win friends.

This is a story of skulduggery in the coursing world and I am persuaded that it is true.

The Brothers had fallen on bad times, or to be more exact they had had an absolutely smashing time, but the old oak chest was sounding pretty hollow. Among the few assets remaining, they had two greyhounds of remarkable ability: Pieman and Pirate, litter brothers, as like as peas in a pod. These the Brothers had kept away from prying eyes. Pieman was entered for the Waterloo Cup, and his sleek form carried all that was left of the Estate. Suffice it to say that the dog won through to the final but only after a semi-final course so tough that no one gave him a chance in the final, and his price lengthened accordingly.

The assembled crowd were amazed by the form of Pieman in the final; he won so convincingly that unless everyone had recognized such a distinctive dog, they would have said that he was totally fresh. So the Brothers cleaned up and went home in triumph, and Pieman and Pirate went home too. I hasten to add that Pieman and Pirate were not the real names of the dogs, so if you have two greyhounds of that name please do not waste your time sueing me.

Mind you, not everyone is as scrupulous as you are. I had a very stirring evening in a pub once with a certain gentleman who had come sadly unstuck over a greyhound. He had gone to Ireland and bought this very high class dog, with a view to cleaning up to some tune at certain flapping tracks.

He began racing the dog regularly, giving it a beefburger or two plus a couple of valium before the race. It will not surprise you to learn that this interesting training regime was most successful in keeping the dog out of the frame, and zooming skywards in the odds. At last, when the dog's handicap was such that anyone would have backed a three-legged sloth against him, an appropriate meeting was selected; the owner's not inconsiderable family were recruited, even unto the second female cousins (thrice removed), and were sent out with handfuls of the folding stuff to shaft all the bookies at the same time. The dog was also prepared: he got firm instructions, a glass of brandy, and two purple hearts.

The bell rang, the hare came round, the traps opened. At the first bend the dog was ten lengths in front; at the second twenty; at the third forty; at the last . . . at the last bend, the dog went straight over the fence, straight through the crowd, and was finally caught three days, and ten miles, later.

The hunting season is well advanced. At the time of writing, we have some eight weeks left, always provided the snow does not return. In most countries spring hunting is a thing of the past. Even in our hills we do not go on much after the first week in April.

I had a foot day in the Crag which is two bits of forest separated by a vertical crag. During the course of the day I conceived it as my duty that I should climb the Crag. The only excuse I can offer is that I had probably been somewhat deranged by the weather. I am not a climber; I get vertigo up a short stepladder. The crag face was covered with snow and ice, and the higher I got the worse it got, with an icy gale blowing round my fundamentals.

I got to the stage when I just knew that I could not get any further up the face, that is until I looked down and reckoned that that looked even worse. I had visions of being crag-fast, and I even started wondering what the Editor would say about me in my obituary. I think that was one of the things that impelled me to the final effort; I am not having him get away with that sort of thing. The other thing that encouraged me was the hand that appeared over the edge of the crag waving a bottle of whisky. The assembled foot followers had recognized my plight, and had hit on the correct stimulus to urge me on. I am now known as 'The Human Fly'.

I am afraid that I have had rather an adverse reaction to my remarks about lady MFHs (*see* pages 95–6). In fact, I was visited by a deputation from BAALAM (British Association of Angry Lady Masters). The deputation was headed by the Madam President herself, Ms Zenobia Streeve-Greebly (MFH, Berkeley Square), her of the Henry Heath hat and sensible brogues at 90°. The ladies and I had full and frank discussions, in which I was required to play little part. They then all went and took tea with Mrs James. I did not take part in this either. I find that being fastened to the stable-door by means of a pitch-fork across the neck rather limits one's activities.

It is a sad thing, and very melancholy, that foxhunters are not the least quarrelsome of Her Majesty's subjects. In fact the only other body of people that I know that have the same capacity for venom are members, and clergy, of the Church (I use the word in the ecumenical sense).

In case you think that I jest, I once attended a garden party, much against my will, and whilst balancing a cup of tea and a rock cake, I listened to a nearby bunch of assorted clergy (a 'chasuble of clergy'?) who were discussing one of their brother clerics *in absentia*; a more thorough hatchet attack on a man's reputation I have seldom been privileged to listen to.

You will notice that I have only mentioned foxhunters amongst the sporting fraternity. This is because those are the only rows that I have experience of. I mean no discourtesy to other branches of sport. I have no doubt that when shooting

syndicates fall out, the resultant blood-letting makes the Lincoln County Cattle Wars look like an Autumn Leaves Outing.

There may well be heroic struggles amongst beaglers; bloody battles at dawn with sinewy legs straining and handfuls of mutton-chop whisker displaced (no doubt the men are just as bad).

But these things I wot not of, but I have had some experience of foxhunters when they cut loose.

I have before me a copy of the *Western Horseman*, the world's leading horse magazine, sent to me by a friend in Canada.

It has some fascinating articles, including 'Branding', 'Making a cow horse', and 'Junior Rodeo'. But it is the adverts that I find riveting. I mean, I'm going to get me a pair of Genuine Peanut Brittle Iguana Boots, some Stetson Cologne, and a genuine pack-mule from Tennessee. But the thing that really fired my imagination was the Roll-o-Roper (make your garage an indoor arena). This consists of a dummy horse on wheels, and a dummy calf, also on wheels. I am unable to make out what the motive power is, but it looks as though the horse has some kind of pedal arrangement and perhaps the calf has some kind of electric motor; or perhaps you have to recruit members of your family to push the various parts about whilst you practise your roping.

I think that this is an absolutely wizard idea, and with a little ingenuity it could be adapted to foxhunting. I see it something like this: a dummy horse for me (motive power, courtesy of Mrs James), an electric hound, radio-controlled by me, and an electric/radio fox controlled as it might be by Master James. Our garage will be an absolute fun palace during the next freeze-up. But I bet I don't catch the fox.

Sometimes when I meet people for the first time, they ask me what I do. If I am feeling perverse I reply either that I am a licensed horse slaughterer, or that I collect pigs' swill. Both are guaranteed conversation stoppers, and no one ever says, 'Gosh, that's really, really super,' although, come to think about it, nothing I say, or do, evokes that sort of response, not even if I say that I write for *Shooting Times*.

However, I was a swill man for a time. I had three months to fill in before taking up my first appointment as an MFH, so I went and signed on at the labour exchange. They sent me to a timber yard. I arrived and reported to the foreman.

'What ho! old bean,' I cried, polishing my gleaming toe-cap up and down the back of my trouser leg, 'I've come about the job.' The foreman was the size and shape of a 300-gallon galvanized water tank. A quick glance suggested that he was a man into whose soul the iron had long since entered, and was rusting quietly there.

He glared at me over the top of the *Daily Mirror* racing page. 'Yerse,' he said. 'Well, when the b——y managing director retires, we'll let you know. Sling yer hook.'

I returned to the labour exchange, and was summoned to see the manager. 'To be frank,' he said, 'I think that you are unemployable.'

I discussed the problem with Paddy and Mick in the Sailor's Farewell that night. Mick said that himself he blamed the students, sure and didn't they cause all the troubles, the students. Paddy said that they had a nice bit of concreting that I could lend them a bit of a hand with. Then Neil came in. Neil had a bit of a pig farm, and wanted someone to drive the swill lorry. So for the next three months I became an assistant swill man.

Four mornings a week we would set off in an ancient lorry, full of rattling bins, and tour a different part of Greater London: hospitals, hotels, restaurants. Every day I shifted three tons of swill bins, developing a pretty robust physique in the process. I had an interesting insight into the underbelly of public catering that left me with a strong determination to stick to home cooking. When you have seen a chef picking his nose over the soup of the day, the definition of 'Chef's Special' takes on a whole new dimension.

I have a new toy. It calls itself an All-Terrain Vehicle, but is in fact a motorized tricycle with huge, globular wheels. It has the great advantage over the motor bike in that it does not fall over the moment my concentration weakens. Because of the huge wheels it is very good on wet ground. I got benighted on the hill with it the other day. After a pretty hairy ride in the dark, I fought through to civilization. The next morning the shepherd tried following my tracks on his motorbike and got bogged good and proper. He was really quite cross about it. The next thing is to train the collies to sit on it.

It is, of course, the very thing for exercising hounds in the summer. George disapproves; he thinks that bicycling is good for fitness (his). Well, that is no problem; I shall chug along on the ATV smoking my pipe, and looking at the day, and he can pedal as hard as he likes in the rear.

We had particularly bad hunting the other day. I apologized to our visitor for this before going home to take it out on Mrs James. He replied that there was no such thing as a bad day's hunting. In the circumstances, I thought that this showed a remarkably well adjusted outlook. But he is right; even being out with hounds is a pleasure and a privilege, a fact that I must remember to point out to the chairman of the Supporters' Club the next time he throws a moody.

We had a poor scenting day recently, but it was the most lovely day, with warm sun and brilliant blue sky. We had a hunt at walking pace, and just riding gently along the hill, watching hounds picking out the line across the valley, was immensely pleasurable.

Hunting in the hills requires a certain amount of terrier work. If a fox goes to ground we try to bolt it. If it will not bolt, then we dig. We had a mammoth 'howk' the other day. Hounds marked at 2.30, and we drew on. I got back to the hole with the hounds at about 5pm. There was no sign of Eric, but shovelfuls of earth kept appearing from the depths, so it looked as though someone was in there. Everyone else had sugared off, proclaiming the place to be hopeless. It was certainly a big place. We got the terrier and the fox out about 7.30; 15 feet down, and 28 feet in to the hill.

How far does your horse carry your lithe and lissom body in the course of a day's hunting? I will bet that you have not the slightest idea. At the end of the February freeze, we met at a certain farm on the hill. The frost was coming out, and on the previous day it looked as though it might be fit for horses. That night there was an iron frost. On the hunting morn, the ground was like concrete with two inches of grease on top. I consulted with Higher Authority, and found the stable doors firmly padlocked, top and bottom. There was nothing else for it but the trike.

So, tucking the terrier down the shirt front, I hacked on to the meet, to be greeted by much ribaldry and many an ill-timed jest from those who had turned out on horses. I am not one of those tiresome people who say I told you so, so I derived no satisfaction from the fact that, separately and severally, they all 'cowped' (turned upside down) during the day.

We had a very busy day, and caught three foxes, all within a two-mile radius of the meet. It was a busy day, but no more than that, and I did no more, and no less, on my tricycle than I would have done on my horse (didn't fall off, though). I clocked up thirty-two miles. This was much further than I would have believed, and if a horse does this sort of mileage on a very average sort of day, what must a hound do? The mileage clocked up by a foxhound in a hill country during the season must be something quite extraordinary.

A year or two back, I was looking for a collie dog which is a bit like trying to find a ham roll in a synagogue. I went to look at one that the owner offered to run for me. There were some blackie hoggs in the field and the dog was set away 'Come by' which, of course, as you all know, means that the dog will do a clockwise run out and beyond the sheep, where it will lie down to await further instructions, or as the advertisements say, it 'will stop to whistle'.

Please do not waste your time writing to me to say that all the shepherds you know use 'Come by' for the anti-clockwise command; some do, some do not, right? Right. Anyway it was

quite academic in this case as the dog hurled himself straight at the centre of the sheep who picked up their skirts and fled. Dog and sheep disappeared over the horizon, pursued by steam engine whistles, and much exhortative blasphemy. A great quiet descended on the scene. I lit my pipe.

Eventually the dog reappeared, grinning happily, but the sheep had obviously taken the hump and declined to accompany him. But then, as his owner pointed out, the dog just lacked a bit of experience; no one could argue with that.

A friend, on a similar mission, had an exactly similar experience. However, on this occasion, just as the hurtling dog was about to cleave through the middle of the scattering sheep, the owner, with great presence of mind yelled out, 'Split 'em!' How's that for quick thinking?

I was told the following story, by the brother-in-law of the man who had met the second cousin of the man whose brother owned the dog, so it must be true. This man bought a dog and discovered that if he threw a stick into the river the dog would run out along the top of the water, pick up the stick, and run back along the top of the water. He sent the dog back. After all, as he said, a dog that could not swim would be no use to him.

Every hunting season I am determined that I will have more days with other people's hounds. At the time of writing I have managed 1.5 days with neighbouring packs. The '.5' took place in a monsoon and hounds went home early, very sensibly.

The '1' happened in hill fog that pretty well negated any chance of seeing anything. All in all, I have not done well, but there never seems to be time. We hunt five days a fortnight, and then the work has to be sandwiched in between. I am quite certain that if I were better organized, I could do better; after all, I know some MFHs who seem to spend more time with other people's hounds than with their own, and if you had ever been out with their hounds, you might understand their restlessness. But it is a good thing to see other hounds and huntsmen. A good pack of hounds will stop you thinking that all your geese are swans, and a bad pack of hounds will confirm you in your prejudices, which is always a comforting thing.

It is also a comfort to see that other huntsmen have trials and tribulations. I am always alert for a new word or a fresh turn of phrase. Not, I hasten to add, that I would ever say that sort of thing, but I do keep a little cellar of vintage, magisterial reprimands, and every now and then I uncork one and roll it round my tongue, just to get the flavour and the bouquet; but I would never dare use one myself.

Mind you, little things do slip out in moments of stress; but that is not quite the same thing. At one stage in my career, I was becoming a nasty, bad-tempered little huntsman. I was saved by my then Hunt Chairman, who blocked my way as I cursed my way down a ride. I can see him now, a small man of great authority, flourishing his whip under my nose, and pointing out that people came out hunting to enjoy themselves, not to be sworn at by a puppy like me. It made a great, and lasting impression on me, and is absolutely true. I do not like being cursed, and so why should anyone else? It does spoil the show.

I have hunted with some real masters of invective but it is self defeating, because if you get cursed every time you open your mouth, then you keep the thing shut, and stop telling the huntsman where you have seen the fox. I remember once galloping across a valley to tell a huntsman where his fox had gone; I took him to the very spot I had last seen it.

'You bloody ——' he snarled. 'It couldn't have gone there.' He then galloped off and his hounds hit off the line of a hare, which I had also seen, and away the silly man went hoicking and tootling. But I had learnt my lesson, and I never helped him again.

By the time you read this I shall be well into, and, I hope well through my lambing. I put the tups in later last back end, because I do not want to be caught with my knickers around my ankles like I was last year. I had it nicely planned that I should start lambing a week after we finished hunting. I also intended to move house in the interval.

At the beginning of the last week of hunting we had twenty-four hours of rain such as you seldom see in this country; there were floods, and my ewes were cut off for a time. There is nothing like a good shower of rain for getting ewes into a maternal mood. The next day was moving day. I went to the sheep early, and there peeping round the side of a great grass tussock was a little white face. It could not be. But it was.

'Go back,' I cried, 'you are ten days early. I have two days' hunting left, and even now the pantechnicon will be demolishing the left-hand gate post.'

But even as I spoke, another ewe started straining. The following ten days is not a period that I look back on with nostalgia. Suffice it to say that the lambs came thick, fast and early (any suggestion that I got my dates wrong will be treated with the contempt that such a suggestion deserves), we moved house, and I got through the last two days' hunting in a sort of coma. I thought it unkind of people to say that they preferred me like that. I got through it and there was quite a good crop of lambs after all that. By the time I should have started, I was nearly finished, and so was the lambing. But it is not an experience that I would care to repeat. I have taken great pains to see that it does not happen this year. It really could not happen again, could it?

I was talking to a friend who herds a hill overlooking a famous beauty spot. He said that he knew that spring had sprung because his hill had sprouted a fresh crop of crisp packets and beer cans. I recently heard a spokesman for the

Ramblers' Association ranting away on the wireless about access to the countryside for his members.

All very fine, but will the Ramblers' Association accept responsibility for the gormless creatures they want to loose on us? Power without responsibility is the historical prerogative of the harlot. The Ramblers want the power to ramble, without taking on themselves any responsibility, so what does that make them? 'Rights' should be a two-way stretch; let the Ramblers ramble by all means, but let them also pay the cost of having their beer cans collected, let them be legally liable for the fences their members knock down, or for the troubles caused by gates left open. Let them put their house in order, then they might find themselves a bit more welcome in the country.

It is interesting to note that, in this part of the world, ramblers are referred to as 'Fell Rats', while in the Lakes they call them 'Plastic Pigs'. I think that if I were a rambler I should be looking to improve my image somewhat.

One of the things that put some people off hunting in the hills is that parts of the hill do tend to be a bit soft or, as they say in the West Country, stuggy. I do not see quite why people get so excited about it; the worst that can happen is that your horse will flounder a bit, and so will you, but at least it is soft falling.

I cut my hunting teeth on Dartmoor – here there are some serious bogs where a horse can founder terminally. They used to say that the difference between Dartmoor and Exmoor was that on Dartmoor you could not ride anywhere except where you could, while on Exmoor you could ride anywhere except where you couldn't: everybody with me so far? Good. There is a story of a man being discovered, on Dartmoor, with just his head sticking out of a bog. On being questioned, he said that he was quite all right, thank you very much, but that he was a bit worried about his horse, on which he was still sitting!

There was, and probably still is, a notorious place on Dartmoor called Black Lane which is a path, of sorts, across a very nasty bit of bog. As I remember, it was only about 18in wide in places, and the path used to bounce up and down as you rode along it, shaking the evil green slime on either side. As the Navy would have said, it was a case of 'Nothing to port, nothing to starboard.' At that time I had a great, and purely intellectual, interest in a young woman who lived at a farm on the other side of the moor. To go and discuss Wittgenstein with her meant a trip of twenty-five miles by road, and petrol had just gone up to some unheard of price, like 2s 9d a gallon.

By the crow, or in my case pony, it was only about ten miles, but it also meant crossing Black Lane. This was not so bad on the outward journey, in daylight, but I did have some interesting moments coming home in the half light of dawn, with very often a nice bit of fog to add spice to the proceedings. I certainly would not do it now, but then I am nothing like as interested in Wittgenstein as I used to be.

I would offer two bits of advice to people not used to the hill. See where the cattle trods are; where they can go, you can usually go on a horse.

If you get lost, remember that every stream flows into a river, and every river, eventually, runs into the sea. So if you try hard enough, you can graduate from being a lost cause on the hill to being a hazard to shipping.

Another useful thing to remember is that it is nearly always colder on the hill than you think it is going to be. I think I am right in saying that every 300 feet in height represents a one degree drop in temperature; add to this the wind-chill factor and you get a very different climate, and a climate that can change for the worse with very little warning.

A member of a mountain rescue team was telling me that they had been called out, in the autumn, to find two missing boys, whom they eventually found suffering from exposure. This was hardly surprising as they had set out in gym shoes and T-shirts with no protective clothing whatsoever!

This is the time of year when the MsFH take up their posts. There are two basic types of MFH: those who have done it before, and those who have not. The experienced, or 'bagman' master is easy to spot. He is on his twelfth pack of hounds; he has seen it all and done most of it. Here he comes driving up to his new kennels in a battered Volvo which contains ten assorted terriers and a plastic suitcase holding his one blue suit, and whatever jewellery he has managed to pinch off his last wife before she went off in high dudgeon, and a horse box with all the furniture. My pearls of wisdom are not for him; cunning lurks in the rheumy eye, and every broken vein on his highly-coloured face is as a campaign medal on an old soldier. Look well, oh ye subscribers, and take your wife's curb chain up another link, and put a new lock on your wine cellar.

He for whom I would unlock the thesaurus of my glittering knowledge, is the New Master. Here he comes in his little Renault 5, a new flat hat on his head, and a song in his heart. He is neat about the neck and feet, and his soul is as pink and shiny as are his downy cheeks; poor little bleeder. Was I ever as hopeful, as innocent, as stupid as that?

The first lesson a newly-minted Master has to learn is that nobody he will meet in the course of his duties will ever say exactly what they mean. Let me give you a few examples:

'My dear chap, as far as I am concerned, you can draw my coverts any time you like; just have a word with my keeper.' If you are lucky you might get to hunt there in February.

'I'm not anti-hunt. I like a bit of hunting. It's these people you get hunting with you these days I can't be doing with.' His neighbour hunts. They fell out over a Blackie tup in 1954.

'Well, you please yourself, sir, you're the Master. But it would never have done for His Late Lordship, sir.' You have absolutely no chance. Once the shades of HLL have been invoked, you have no hope of getting your way.

'A little bit of a problem at the kennels, sir; if you could pop over.' This is serious, and could mean anything from bubonic plague to the second whipper-in carving himself a round off one of the female stable persons, in the firm's time. The first problem would be easier to sort out.

'I'm afraid that boring old George is away racing, but do come in and have a little drinkie.' Ay! Ay! stand by to repel boarders. Well actually, I have to admit that I have never really encountered this problem. I am one of those people who always remind ladies of their Dear Old Uncle Toby, and while they are very happy to pour out their troubles to me, they have never seemed very enthusiastic about my adding to them. However, if you want to spend all summer having your ear nibbled instead of attending to your duties, that is a matter of personal choice, and no concern of mine, however much I may deplore your behaviour. I mean, I do not for one moment want you to think that I am jealous, I am only thinking of your moral welfare, and the good name of the hunt. Who made that rude noise?

As a new, and quite possibly nubile, person, the new Master will not lack for invitations to browse, and, if he is lucky, sluice. However, these are not always what they seem. I well remember, in my first season, receiving an invitation to dine from a jovial member of the field. On the appointed night I presented myself, properly attired, at the correct place of residence. I was met on the doorstep by Mrs Anything But Jovial Member of the Field. The burthen of her complaint (*fortissima*) was that 'No one had told her that I was coming she had only just got back from visiting her mother and there was absolutely nothing to eat in the house unless I had some cornflakes, but that if I did then the wretched children would have to go without their breakfast!'

This is absolutely a true story, but I may say that I have only given a pale and bowdlerized version of the original. During the brief pauses for breath that the lady allowed herself, I could hear (stage left) the unmistakeable noises of a jovial member of the field taking on board yet another restoring draught. It was quite obvious that I was redundant to the scene of domestic harmony that was about to be enacted, so I made my excuses and left.

As I was jolly hungry, I stopped for fish and chips on the way home. If you want to take part in an interesting social experiment, try standing in a queue for fish and chips wearing a velvet smoking jacket; you will not lack for sauce, or vinegar.

5

The house is wracked with internal strife. Mrs James and I communicate only by note of hand and grunts. Suspicion, and mistrust, are rife. The problem stems, as do most problems in our house, from animals, in this case the dogs.

We have five dogs: two operational collies, a superannuated collie and two miscellaneous. The troubles emanate from the miscellaneous. For many years the house was ruled by the Fraggle. The Fraggle owns Mrs James, and is a mixture of dandy dinmont, Yorkshire terrier, cairn, and wire-haired dachshund. He is a useless, but engaging, chap, who only thinks of two things, the other one being rabbits. He actually caught a rabbit once, and was totally bemused by this unexpected turn of affairs. In fact, it was rather like that time the Blankshire caught a fox; anyone here old enough to remember that?

The even tenor of the Fraggle's ways continued for some years. Then one day Jessica Jane arrived. JJ as she will hereinafter be referred to, is a Patterdale. A Patterdale is an off-shoot of the Lakeland terrier. When JJ came she was the size, and shape, of a coal-black tennis ball. The Fraggle decided that it was his mission in life to bounce the tennis ball on every possible occasion. There would be snarls, snaps, shrieks of woe, and not a little inconvenience for me because, if I was sitting in my chair, JJ would scrabble up and seek sanctuary by sitting on top of my head. I well remember pointing out to the Fraggle, at the time, that, in common with all repressors, he was laying the seeds for future problems.

So it has come to pass. JJ has just finished her first working season. She has assisted in the eviction of over twenty foxes. Although small to look upon, she is 15lb of wire and whipcord, with all the charm and sensitivity of a chainsaw. The storm broke when she caught the Fraggle investigating her dish (empty). Even my powers of purple prose are unable to do justice to the upset that followed. Suffice it to say that she yokked the Fraggle. The Fraggle is at least twice the size of JJ, but when, at last, I managed to grab her up, the Fraggle came too, by an ear. It was a horrid scene: Mrs James was screaming, the Fraggle was screaming, I was saying one or two things like '*%*', and '–°**'. 'Well, after all, my after-breakfast pipe was being disturbed.) The only silent one was JJ partly because I was throttling her, but mainly because her mouth was full of Fraggle. Eventually there was a nasty tearing sound, and the Fraggle dropped off, minus one or two non-essential pieces.

At this, JJ let fly a flow of such appalling invective that I had to ask Mrs James to leave the room. Since then relations in our household have been strained. The moral of this story is that if you want to stick your nose in someone else's dish, make sure it does not belong to a small, black Patterdale terrier.

Let it not be said that we shy away from confronting the major problems of our time in this column. We are not afraid to face up to such things as racial prejudice: like the man who said that there were two things that he really hated – one was racial prejudice, the other was foreigners.

We were all gathered in the Jolly Knackerman, the other day, when John came in. Some good-natured banter was exchanged about him being allowed out etc, etc. The point was, he said, that his wife had taken to her bed with a migraine. So we all said we were terribly sorry, and bought him a drink. Eugene was sitting in the corner, and the situation was obviously worrying him. At last he spoke. 'Tell me,' he said, 'this Migraine. What part of the world would he come from?'

The Land Agents are having a bad time. They all tell me so, and who am I to disbelieve them. In fact I saw one wearing black wellies the other day, so things must be coming to a pretty pass. One of their problems is that they have a lot of farms to sell, but the purchasers are no longer pounding at the office door, slobbering to be let in. This means that the Agents are straining at their leashes, seeking to lay hold of any suitable customer. Stroll down Land Agents' Row at any major agricultural show, and you will be continuously importuned by unshaven, blear-eyed fellows in patched corduroys and ragged tweeds. If you show the slightest sign of weakness, they will whip out sheaves of well-thumbed particulars, with garish photographs of profitable beef/arable holdings, with desirable Georgian residences, in the most compromising positions.

This eagerness can lead the lads into unfortunate situations. You can imagine the fluttering in the Land Agents' dovecote, at a certain major show, when it was bruited about that there were two Genuine Bedouin on the loose, with their jellabas

stuffed with petro-dollars which they wished to invest in a large country estate. Sure enough there they were, two dusky gentlemen in burnouses and very dark glasses. They were made very welcome indeed. They passed from stand to stand, to the frenetic popping of champagne corks for, strange to relate, these sons of the desert seemed less than enthusiastic about the strictures of the Koran on the consumption of alcohol. In fact, their consumption was quite fearful. It gradually began to dawn on the assembled Chartered Surveyors that all was not quite as it should be. It was a hot day, such as to make people sweat, and the dusky faces were getting a bit stripey. The shekel finally dropped when the two sheikhs reeled up to yet another stand with their arms round each other, making a fairly unsuccessful attempt at the 'Rose of Tralee'.

They may not yet have discovered how to get oil out of the ground in Co Tipperary, but they certainly know how to take the wine out of the Chartered Surveyors.

I have spent a large part of my life sitting on horses getting wet and cold, and so it is hardly surprising that, as I approach the male menopause, parts of the body have started to complain a bit. I have a lot of trouble from an arthritic neck. For fellow sufferers, may I recommend that they try New Zealand Green-Lipped Mussel pills. They are available at any decent chemist, and they have certainly made a big difference to me.

As we seem to be on the subject of dampness, I remember calling on a man who had recently moved into the neighbourhood. It was a large house, with an extensive stable block. I was rather surprised to see that he was building some new stables, and asked him why. It was all quite simple. He thought that the old stables were much too damp for horses, so he was having them converted into a flat for his mother-in-law.

The trouble with the world today is that there are too many 'caring' people about. 'Caring' is a word that has fallen on hard times (like 'gay'). Caring has become the battle cry of all those who seek to mask their own inadequacies by interfering in the affairs of others, usually with disastrous results. But I must not let my feelings wax too hot in a family paper. *Shooting Times* is not the place to suggest that the world would be a better place if all sociologists were rendered down into soap. I will content myself with an example of the havoc that can result from an over-developed social conscience.

A certain man went forth in a Land-Rover, and lo, as he journeyed he chanced to come upon a concrete block lying in the road. 'Verily,' he said to his caring self, 'here lies a hazard for the unwary traveller.' So he stopped the Land-Rover, got out, and moved the block to the side of the road. Then he dusted his hands, and with the glow of righteousness warming his soul he turned back to his vehicle.

The vehicle had gone.

There were two good reasons for the disappearance. 1: he had left the vehicle on the crown of a hill. 2: he had neglected to engage the handbrake. It was a long straight hill that led down to the village and to a bend on which stood a butcher's shop. The driverless Land-Rover trundled down the hill and, ignoring the corner, embedded itself in the butcher's plateglass window. The moral of this story is obvious, but in case you are of too little wit to see it, it is neatly encapsulated in that famous old Devon proverb:

'Let concrete block bide where 'tis tu, and you won't spoil the butcher's vu.'

I found a photograph of the Younger James at the helm of a governess cart, or as they were known where I was bred and buttered, a jingle. Those were the days of petrol rationing, and the car, a Vauxhall 14, and its keeper Roy were called out only on special occasions. I suppose I must have learnt to drive a pony quite naturally, in the same way that I thought nothing of walking distances that would make me flinch a bit today, and which my son would never have considered that it was possible to walk. I suppose that if I put my mind to it I could still put the harness on a horse, but I think I would have to learn to drive again from scratch.

If I had the time, and money, I would set up a smart cob and a dog cart. I still have my Grandfather's driving coat. It is a truly magnificent garment, ankle length and velvet collared, and made of material so heavy and thick that it will almost stand up by itself.

As well as the jingle there was a four-wheeled dog cart and a landau, both quietly gathering dust. The only time I ever rode in the landau was on its final journey to a farm sale. Bob hooked his motor bike between the shafts and towed it off with me aged five sitting in the back like a duke, or a lord, waving regally to every South Devon cow whose attention I could attract. I expect that it was sold for shillings, and wonder what it would be worth today.

George bought a lot of his coaches for shillings. George is a very canny man, and had the foresight, after the war, to buy up the redundant horse-drawn vehicles that were being practically given away as scrap. As a result he now has one of the finest collections of HDVs in the country. He puts them to work. If you see a stage coach, or a Hansom cab on the telly, it is a guinea to a gooseberry that they belong to George. Did you know that there are only three Hansom cabs still in existence? And if memory serves me right, he has two of them.

His collection of carriages, of all types, must be very valuable indeed, and the great thing is that they still work. He had a dog cart that really took my fancy. It had belonged to a Master of the Cottesmore, and was all fitted out as a terrier vehicle, with boxes for the terriers, and a place for the tools.

George once allowed me to take the ribbons of a four-in-hand. I can still remember the tremendous feeling of latent power that four horses transmit along the reins, and I can absolutely understand the fascination that people find in driving.

Many years ago I was driving through Buckinghamshire, which is the sort of rather stupid thing one does when young. I rounded a corner and came upon the late Nubar Gulbenkian out for a drive; it was the most splendid sight. The whole thing was absolutely immaculate. A pair of slashing greys, a marvellous bottle-nosed groom up behind, with the arms correctly folded; everything shining, and polished to the nth degree. I stopped, raised my hat, and the old man saluted me gravely with his whip. It is always a pleasure to see something really well done, and my mini van felt very scruffy, and tinny, when I got back into it.

I have been camping in a caravan for the lambing. It is a neat little thing and its proud owner maintains that it will sleep four people. It is not for me to dispute his claim, but I can say that it certainly would not sleep four of James. I did live in a caravan for a year, in my youth, but that was a much more substantial affair. It had a little coke stove that would only stay in at night if you got up at three and stoked it, and a separate bedroom. I lived in it all through the notorious winter of 1962/63, and I can well remember that when I woke up in the morning my moustache would be frozen solid; happy days.

The Holiday is looming up. Left to my own devices it is doubtful whether I would stir out of Northumberland, except for the trip to London to buy the annual shirt. But Mrs James will brook no argument, and so it will be Ho for the Costa Blanca where I will perform a son's duty to visit his mother.

I had a stab at foreign travel as a young man. I felt that there must be something in it that I was missing, and that it was somehow wrong to be content with my animals, my pipe and my armchair at home. I discovered what most people discover, but do not dare to admit, that travel is usually either boring and uncomfortable, or full of anxiety and uncomfortable. In either case, you certainly do not want to pay out wads of the folding stuff for it.

After all if I want to be bored and uncomfortable, all I have to do is to go down the road and hunt with the Blankshire. For true anxiety there is nothing to beat a visit to the Bank Manager. But if you really want the James award for a country that you will be really pleased to get out of, and which will supply a generous measure of anxiety, boredom and discomfort, the buttered teacake must go to Colonel Gaddafi's Libya, and all you can get to help things along is Coca-Cola, or grape juice.

At least I can get a dram in my armchair.

We are having a musical evening in aid of the hunt. I was musing about it the other day, and it occurred to me that there was a great dearth of hunting songs. The honourable exception to this is the Lake District where there is a great tradition of songs about famous hunts and huntsmen. Outside the Lakes the only hunting song that I can think of is the Devon and Somerset song. I think that this is a sad state of affairs. What about a competition for some new hunting songs? Such pithy titles as 'Llandeilo Farmer's Lament' (the latter to be sung by a massed male voice choir) spring to mind. There is already a tune called the Morpeth Rant; no doubt some of the subscribers will be able to think up some suitable words to go with it. All contributions to be rendered in a nasal tenor, with the eyes tight shut, and a pint glass firmly clutched in the right hand.

We could have the final judging in the ring at Peterborough;

it might even prevent the junior Master of the West Percy from going to sleep after luncheon.

How much are we affected by our environment? I am quite certain that where we live and work must have a profound effect on the way we look at life. I am fortunate in that the 'lines have fallen unto me in pleasant places', and I am therefore rightly noted for my sunny disposition; to be otherwise would be base ingratitude. To live in squalor, and be miserable, can hardly be unexpected, but to be a miserable duke is a crime against humanity, and such people had better move over and let me do the job: I should be an immensely jolly duke. Someone once said that the German character, with its tendency to hysteria and cruelty, was shaped by 'a thousand miles of screaming forest'. I can well believe this. You only have to meet forestry workers in this country who spend their working lives in a dank, coniferous gloom, to find that the chill of the forest has entered into their souls. They tend to be very different from the average farmworker whose work is in the open.

I have never worked in a factory, but I am certain that it would make me pretty bloody-minded and, the larger the concern and the more boring the work, the more likely I would be to come out on strike, to break the monotony and to demonstrate to myself, and others, that I was still a person and not a statistic.

Climate affects us too. The native of Aberdeen will approach life in a different way from the native of Skibereen. Generations of granite and biting east winds drive a man to prodigies of commercial effort, if only because to cease work for any length of time would mean freezing up, and the eventual loss of bodily appendages.

If you can see the hills in Skibereen it means that it is about to rain and therefore not worth starting work. If you cannot see the hills, this will be because it is raining already. In either case the best thing is to hold your hour, and have another; if it does not get done today, then it will get done tomorrow; and it might now, Michael, so it might.

As a Cornishman, I was raised in rain-sodden lassitude and am spiritually closer to Cork than Aberdeen. As to Work Ethic, I had ten bob each way the last time it ran at Kempton, and the blighter is running yet. I will make a start on the jobs tomorrow, and I might now, Michael, so I might; providing it does not rain, of course.

I have been giving some thought to declining. I have taken this word from an advertisement that a friend told me about in a Hereford paper. The advert was for a farm sale; all the usual things from bulls to balers, and 'sundry small tools'. The sale was on the orders of Mr X 'who was declining farming'. I thought that that was a lovely phrase.

I am now starting my twentieth season as a Master-huntsman. This is not so bad, considering the fact that everybody told me that it was out of the question that I should ever be able to hunt hounds; that I was too fat, and too impoverished. When I look back now, I realize that everybody was quite right; by any sensible yardstick I should never have become an MFH. The only trouble was that I did not realize it at the time, and here I am, half my lifetime later, still floundering about the countryside. But I realize that I cannot go on for ever. I am getting fatter and slower. I would no longer wish to hunt hounds four days in the week, as used to be my ambition, and perhaps when the conditions are bordering on the nasty, I do not make the same decision that I would have done ten years ago, as to whether it is huntable or not.

With a few honourable exceptions, nearly every amateur huntsman goes from ability to disability, and sometimes to dotage, before they can be persuaded to give up. How many times has one heard it said: 'Poor old b—r, you should have seen him when he was really going; it's pathetic to watch him now.' Of course, they are quite right. People who pay for their hunting are entitled to expect a reasonable return for their outlay, and geriatrics, however talented they once may have been, will not deliver the goods. Every huntsman knows the problems that can be caused by good old doghounds who have got slow and jealous: there is only one answer for that case, and the Master should mark the lesson well.

I hope that I have learnt that lesson. I like to think that I have got a season or two yet, but I have every intention of 'declining hunting' before it declines me.

By now the hunt changes will have had time to settle down a bit. All the new huntsmen will be getting a little bored of telling people what a filthy state their predecessor left the kennels in, but not half as bored as the people will be of listening to it. If I may presume to offer a little advice to all incoming Masters and hunt servants, it is this. Never vilify the previous administration; if it was a bad one, it is much better if you let the country tell you so and, if you are half about the job, compare you favourably to those who have gone before. If your predecessor was a better man than you, and stranger things have been known to happen, then, by running him down, you will quickly demonstrate to the country what a complete twit you in fact are. And if I were you I would conceal that fact for as long as I could. It will not be long.

Whether you bred your new Master yourself or imported him can be a decision of great importance, and there are pros and cons in both cases.

On the face of it, the home-bred Master is the best bet. After all he (or she) knows the country, and knows the people. That, at least, is the theory, but sadly life is not like that. I was once hunting with a man who had been Master in the same country for some twenty years. He never knew where he was out hunting and could not remember the name of any farmer

who lived more than a mile from his own house. But he was a charming man.

It is a great help to know everybody in the country, but by the same token they know all about you, and in some cases they know a lot more than you think or would care to know that they know, if you know what I mean. A home-bred Master must indeed have lived a life of saint-like chastity and probity for no one in the country to be able to rattle even a small chest of bones. However, if the Master has been far-sighted enough to sow all his wild oats away from home, then no one will mind so much.

Another disadvantage that the home-bred model suffers from is that, if he lives in a country where internecine strife is endemic, then he will by birth or environment be involved. By virtue of this fact, everything that he does as Master will be judged, not on its own merits, but by the standards of clan loyalty.

However, I suggest that if you can find someone in the country who can command the respect of the majority of the people, and can find his way about the place without getting himself, and everybody else lost, then I should look no further.

The alternative is the Import. First find your Import. This is not easy. You can advertise in the trade papers, and you will get a flood of replies. It is possible that there may be a nugget among them. It is a sad fact that foxhunting is a difficult and demanding trade, and that many who long desperately to take a pack of hounds would do neither themselves, nor hunting, much good if they did.

Hunting is a small world. Everybody knows, or knows about, everybody else. It is not difficult to check the credentials of any possible Import, always supposing that you can find one. What you are seeking is an UMM (Upwardly Mobile Master), or even a DOMM (the opposite). They are in very short supply, and indeed may be on the verge of extinction.

The MM has one great advantage: he comes fresh to a country and has no local axes to grind. He has a chance of uniting all local factions, even if it be in a united desire to slide him down the road on his ear.

The MM has another advantage. If he is at all capable, he will have hunted in different places, and gained experience with different packs in different places. The home-bred Master has very often never hunted anywhere except from home, and never seen any pack of hounds except the home team. However good the home team is, it is always healthy to see other teams play, and other ways of doing the job. To choose the right way, a man must know some different ways from which to choose. There is a certain amount to be said for the imported Master, provided that he is reasonably capable, and that he eschews all drunkenness, fornication, lewdness, intemperate language, riotous behaviour, and always gets the horses home by three o'clock. Though why anybody should want a miserable blighter like that beats me.

I am not one for informal dress. Even when I go on holiday, sartorial conventions have to be observed. However, for the sojourn in Spain, Grimling unbent so far as to include a linen jacket and some flannels in the luggage, and even suggested that a shirt with a soft collar might be permissible. Imagine my consternation, on arriving at Alicante, to find that the luggage had not bothered to leave Heathrow. The Harris tweed suit, the tackety shoes and the horn heid stick, all of which are obligatory at Newcastle aerodrome, began to weigh somewhat heavily upon my soul in the claggy heat of southern Spain.

One of the sad things about the Spanish is that they still believe that the individual is more important than the state. They have not yet experienced the enlightened benefits produced by comprehensive maleducation, and top-heavy bureaucracy. Thus it is with regret that I have to announce that Iberia sent a van with my case to Mother's doorstep, seventy miles from the airport, the very next morning. I wonder if British Airways would have been guilty of such reactionary, and anti-social behaviour? I do not thnk that I shall take a chance on it. Next time I shall send Grimling, and the luggage, down by an earlier plane.

I have mentioned the shepherds' suppers that take place in this part of the world, and the marvellous singers, story-tellers, and musicians who entertain at them. It has long been a bone of contention with the ladies of the Hunt that, because the suppers are only attended by members of the weaker sex, they never get to hear these entertainers. So last night we had a musical evening in aid of the Hunt. It was magic. One hundred and fifty people came, and for a quid they had a menu of some of the finest singers in the Borders (yes, I did sing, and, no, I am not talking about myself); the Duke of Northumberland's piper; some story-tellers, who my neighbour said were better than anything you get on the telly; the best mouth organ player in the country, and a fiddler and accordionists who are not only famous in this country but throughout the world.

The dramming, the singing and the crack went on into the full light of dawn. Then the Chairman of the Supporters' Club, the Vice-Chairman and I danced barefoot in a fairy ring, in the dewy grass. You think I jest? As I said it was a magic evening, so almost anything might have happened, and very likely did.

June is the time of year when, occasionally, I leave the nest and go to stay with people (seldom the same people twice for some strange reason). One of the rituals that I try to avoid is the visitors' book. It brings out the worst in me, and I yearn to write things like, 'Quoth the Raven . . .' and 'The piece of cod that passeth all understanding'. Sometimes I give in to the urge, and have to cross another billet off my list.

At one such place I found the visitors' book open at a particular page, which I assumed must be meant for me, as there was only one other entry on the page. It was a large signature and consisted of just a christian name, and a residence that appeared to be not a million miles from the town of Windsor. I took the other half of the page, and wrote 'James, Northumberland' across it. I still do not understand why the hostess was so upset; I mean, I had not even included one of my comments; ah well, there's nowt so queer as folk.

The compulsory period for dipping against sheep scab is approaching, and I shall be very involved this year. I have invested in a mobile dipper and I am taking to the roads with it, all in the name of increased cash flow. Thoughts about dipping have reminded me of the 'Lent Sheep'. What, you may ask, is a lent sheep? I will tell you.

I got the story from an old friend of mine, now sadly fallen off the perch. Just after the last war my friend bought a farm on the edge of Dartmoor. My friend was new to the area and to farming, and so was pleasantly surprised when his neighbour called in and offered to dip his sheep for him. 'Just send the boy over with them tomorrow.' So he did.

He was again pleasantly surprised when, a few days later, another neighbour called with a similar offer. My friend said how kind, but the sheep had already been dipped. It would, said the neighbour, do them all the good in the world to be dipped again. So once more the boy set forth.

When the third neighbour came with a similar offer, my friend was truly touched by the generous behaviour of the Dartmoor farmers; neighbour three simply would not take no for an answer. When the fourth offer of a free dip came my friend felt that there was something in the air apart from the, by now, rather pervasive odour of sheep dip. This time he went with the boy and the sheep. There seemed to be an awful lot of sheep gathered to dip, and there were farmers one, two and three, plus Bill Brewer, Jan Stewer, Peter Gurney, and full supporting cast. There also was the man from the Ministry, who was supervising the dip and also counting the sheep through, for it was on the count through the dip that the hill sheep subsidy was eventually paid out. A few days later my friend notified the Ministry of his intention of dipping his sheep; he also notified Peter Davey, Dan'l Whiddon, 'arry 'awk, Old Uncle Tom Cobbleigh, and all. And that, my dears, is what was meant by 'Lent Sheep'.

I stand corrected, and humiliated. In a recent article I used a rude Latin phrase (a) because I wanted to show off, and (b) because I wanted to see if I could get away with it. I did not. The Editor, hawk-eyed classicist that he is, leapt upon it with a cry of rage and a blue pencil, and substituted a somewhat humbler vulgarity in the vernacular. However, I am undaunted; I will attempt once more to raise the cultural tone of this column. Are you ready? Then here goes: 'Sic Transit Gloria', which as you all know means: 'Gloria has chucked up in the van again'. By Jove, I feel better for that – and I expect that Gloria does too.

I am feeling especially sensitive about things urban because I have just been on the annual trip to London. For various reasons, with which I will not bore you, I was forced to catch a commuter train to Euston. When I tell you that the last time I travelled on a commuter train it was pulled by a steam engine, then you will appreciate that I experienced something of a culture shock. If I travelled animals the way that BR travels commuters, then I would fully expect to be prosecuted. It was a shocking experience to a gentle soul like myself. Not only was there no room to open my paper, but the large man who came and hung over my seat had obviously dined with more enthusiasm than judgment the previous night, and I suspect that baked beans and keg beer had figured largely on the menu.

It was, therefore, a James in pretty tatty fettle who staggered into Jermyn Street that morning. I enjoy Jermyn Street. It is there that I buy the Annual Shirt, and the Annual Bottle of Aftershave. I also enjoy looking in all the shops, at all the things that no one could possibly want to buy, but I must presume that somebody actually does. There is also a jolly tobacconist where they have little holders that you stick on the dashboard of your car, to put your pipe in. I bought one, as a present for the tractor this year.

As an extra treat I went to a well-known hatters and bought myself a new flat hat. I know that all you keen young Sloane Rangers like these modern, streamlined flat hats, but I favour the good old, full-blown, dog poisoner type of cap that only the well-known hatter still supplies.

I am going to look at a horse on Monday. So what? I hear you say. A simple enough operation, do it all the time. Not like I do you don't. It is generally accepted that I am incapable of buying a postage stamp properly on my own, let alone a horse. So HOJLAC was formed. HOJLAC stands for the Horses for James Ladies' Advisory Committee. It consists of the lady Joints, the lady whipper-in and Mrs James, and you just think on that for a moment.

Now imagine that you are your average run-of-the-mill, friendly, neighbourhood horse dealer; you spend your peaceful days dreaming of schemes by which you may do good to the public, and generally spread a little happiness about the place. There you are dreaming your dreams, and trying to sell a nice 16.3BG perfectgent quiet clip, shoe, box (and for all you know, it might be), suit MFH (or nervous lady), a genuine 8 (and it must be a very genuine 8 because it has been the same age for the last five years, and so it must be used to it by now).

There you are, you perspicacious purveyor of palfreys, looking forward to entering a nice mug punter, and round the corner and into your yard march HOJLAC. As an interested spectator at many of these encounters, I cannot but feel some compassion for these unfortunate men when confronted with such a body of lovely but formidable ladies. It is pitiable indeed to watch a grown man quailing as those merciless eyes and fingers lay bare all the faults and blemishes on the star of the stable (such a nasty shock for the poor man too, to find that his expensive horse has all those nasty things wrong with it). The haggling over the price is always the difficult part of a deal, but that is when the lady whipper-in produces that bit of rubber hose that she keeps stuck in her boot, and – but no, I really cannot bring myself to tell you any more.

I detect a sinister movement in the puppy show circuit. I have made it quite plain in these columns that if anyone wants me to come and make comments of a coruscating brilliance about their hounds, then I expect to be given lunch beforehand. I will not adorn their puppy judging unless I am browsed and sluiced beforehand. I mean surely they are not stupid enough to think that anyone *wants* to come and look at their absolutely ghastly hounds.

I will have nothing to do with this curmudgeonly behaviour. As long as I am a Master, our puppy show will take place after luncheon, and if one of the Joint-Masters insists on giving the meal, then the least that I can do is to give in gracefully. As a matter of principle I will not be attending any evening puppy shows; after all, I might miss 'Coronation Street'.

I have also noticed a distressing tendency to forget the glass of port after luncheon. Now I am not an unreasonable man; I know that belts have had to be tightened, etc, etc. Of course I realize that you cannot offer decent port to all the dreadful people you feel it necessary to clutter up your luncheon with, but that is no excuse for depriving me of the restoring draft. No, the thing to do is to shut me, and one or two other choice spirits, in the library, with the decanters, and forget about us; we will look after ourselves, and will land at the show nicely in time for a cup of tea. That way you will avoid the trauma of having us sitting at the ringside criticizing your hounds, in loud, and oh so carrying, voices.

The foxhound is a remarkable animal. A senior foxhunter of my acquaintance says that you can teach them to do almost anything except write the meet cards, and he is working on that. Some years ago I went to a show and watched a certain pack of hounds parading. The huntsman took the hounds into the centre of the ring, put them up together, and rode out of the ring without a backward glance. Not a hound moved. The huntsman then reappeared at the other end of the ring, touched his horn, and all the hounds galloped gladly to him. It was well done, and impressive, although not difficult if you are prepared to spend the time to achieve it. The man I was standing next to dismissed the whole thing as 'damned circus tricks', and of course I agreed with him – I agreed with everybody in those days.

A few years later I went out with a pack of hounds in the West Country. They marked a fox to ground in a field bank. The terriers arrived, and the huntsman took hounds well back into the middle of the field. The excavations did not seem to be going well, so the huntsman left his hounds in the middle of the field, no one with them, and came to enthuse the diggers; not a hound moved, until the fox finally bolted. I thought that was a useful application of a circus trick, and a fine example of control.

Control is a very necessary thing with hounds. Anyone who wants to take sixty, or seventy, hounds for a walk needs to exert a modicum of control. It can be overdone.

When I was a young man there was a school of thought that, when out of the kennel, hounds should be rigidly confined behind the huntsman at all times. This is manifest nonsense, for apart from being very boring for hounds and men, hounds will learn absolutely nothing except a detailed knowledge of their huntsman's rear view, and even that must begin to pall after a bit. They will not find, or catch, many foxes from that position either although there are huntsmen who would disagree with me on this matter.

In fact there are huntsmen to whom a pack of hounds must be a positive encumbrance. They obviously know so much more than their hounds about where the fox has gone that one really wonders why the hunt goes to all the trouble and expense of keeping such stupid animals. Still, they do look pretty at the meet.

Hound exercise is upon me. Every year I meet some poop who tells me how much he enjoys hound exercise. I sat and listened, one night, to one of these clowns waxing lyrical about the dew on the grass, the snail on the thorn, and the tweeting of the birds. 'But do you not get fed up with it after six weeks solid?' I asked. He looked at me as though I was stupid (well, people do). 'I only go once a year,' he said.

For twenty years I went five days a week for six to eight weeks: bowler hats, collar and tie, old red coat, top boots without spurs; one, two, three, four hours a day. In most countries, there are only so many routes available for exercise and, however scenic they may be, they will start to pall after a bit. It is quite fun to begin with, but after six weeks, hounds, men and horses have had hound exercise right up to here. At this point the weather breaks, hounds are popping out of their skins, there is obviously a roaring scent, and every sodden cornfield that you pass obviously contains wall-to-wall foxes.

Masters of hounds tend to experience something of a sense of humour failure at this time of year. Should the wife of the MFH have some negative feedback to impart to her Lord and Master at this time of year; should she, for instance, bend the horsebox, or find that she is pregnant by the ginger milkman, then I suggest that she arranges a hasty visit to her mother, and telephones the glad tidings from there. An eminent huntsman once said that he considered that hound exercise was as hard work as cubhunting, but none of the fun.

My tricycle is an excellent machine for exercising hounds, and I am using it extensively this year. Third gear in the reduced box is just a nice hound jog. The main drawback is that you can only carry your whip in your left hand.

A huntsman was having some difficulty with his new and none too bright whipper-in on hound exercise. 'Now listen, Jack, when a car comes up behind shout "Car behind" and drop your whip to get the hounds over.' Now we all know that dropping the whip means letting the thong hang down to keep the hounds into side. Here comes a car.

'Car behind,' sings out Jack. The car passes the hounds, but there is a nasty crunch: 'What's that?' says the huntsman. 'Please sir, I dropped my whip like you said, and the car's run over it.'

I had hoped to start hunting earlier than usual this year. The splendid cubhunting cob which I bought last year is a horse of great charm and character. He came in from the hill a month ago, and now he has gone finally, and irrevocably, lame. This is a great blow. I know that someone is going to write to me and say that they got their horse in from grass one day, and went hunting the next morning; the answer to that is not on the hills they did not. A horse has to be in for at least six weeks before one can consider taking it hill hunting. Even in the autumn, hill hunting can be an on-going situation. Two seasons ago, in early September, we had a hunt of twenty-three miles, with a 7-mile point. I do not think that the horse you dragged out of the field yesterday would have got you very far.

There was something on the wireless (we have never got round to getting a radio) about dowsing. You will all know that dowsing is the method of detecting water or minerals below ground. I believed in dowsing. I believe in all that sort of thing, even fairies. I had never seen any dowsing until a year or two ago. We had lost a drain on the farm. You know how it is, you lay something down for a second and somebody picks it up and takes it off somewhere to use it for something that it was never intended for in the first place, usually bending it in the process.

Everybody knew that this drain was on the farm, but nobody knew where it was. Then Percy rolled up. Percy was a man of many talents that included electric wiring. He was, he said, a dowser, and would find the drain, no bother. He did, with a twisted wire coat-hanger. He made me try it. I did not know where the drain was to the nearest 100ft, but I found it with the coat-hanger. There was no doubting the quite definite downward pull of the coat-hanger when I crossed the drain. It was not violent, just a firm downward pressure; there was no denying it.

I have never had the occasion to dowse since. Indeed, I must admit to being somewhat worried by the powers hidden deep inside me. But I might be prepared to demonstrate these forces for a reasonable consideration. If you invite me round with my coat-hanger, I will guarantee to find your whisky, in the time it takes you to say, 'I'm terribly sorry but we have not got a drop in the house.'

'Hubris' is defined, in the *Concise Oxford Dictionary* as 'insolent pride'. I rather suspect that most MsFH develop hubris, to a greater or lesser extent, from time to time. It comes from all the bowing and scraping one has to put up with, everybody getting up when you enter the room and all that sort of thing.

It's a frightful bore really, but the trouble is that one gets rather used to it after a bit, and one can become quite shirty if no one rushes to light one's cigarette, or if some damn long-haired woofter contradicts some amazingly wise and clever pearl that you have condescendingly tossed to the assembled swine.

Of course, *I* am not like that. I am much too level-headed to be carried away by the magnificence of my posiiton. I do not regard my near perfection as a matter to boast about; it just happens to be the way I am. However, I know that lesser mortals do tend to get carried away, so let me offer a surefire antidote to hubristic tendencies.

Take yourself to one of the local shows and go and lean against the bar for the last hour before the barman starts packing up the glasses. You are then certain to meet a large section of hunt supporters – or not, as the case may be. They will all be most happy to allow you to buy them a drink, and, once the drink is safely over the tonsils, to impart much interesting information to you.

Let us consider the case of an average hunt supporter. His day has not been a success. His dog has made a horlicks of the sheepdog trial; the judge put up a gimmer that a child could see was not a patch on the one exhibited by the supporter (but then the judge is married to the winner's second cousin . . .); one of the bairns has thrown up in the car, and the wife's mother is coming to stay for a week.

The HS is a man in whose body there is normally a generous dollop of the milk of human kindness slopping about but, throughout the day, the milk has been well mixed with copious drafts of ale and whisky, and by 4pm the whole nasty mixture is starting to curdle in the gut and mental and physical dyspepsia is setting in.

The only thing to do is to attend once more upon the beer tent, and, Hooray, there leaning against the bar is the MFH, smirking all over his great fat, red face; now is the moment to go and tell him all the things that you have been longing to tell him all season . . .

It is a salutary time for the MFH. In an hour, he will buy an immense amount of whisky, and in return he will be accused of rape, aggravated assault, being a rotten huntsman, GBH, breaking and entering, riding a horse whilst under the influence and industrial espionage. He will ask for twenty-three other offences to be taken into consideration. He will be tried, summarily convicted and fined an immense amount of whisky.

If the MFH's hubris can survive all that, then he has thrown a double six and becomes the next leader of any political party.

My Northumbrian language coach has expressed qualified approval at my progress. I have been taking lessons for some time, and intend to continue until such times as Mrs James finds out about it all.

Perhaps you would like to try one of the elementary exercises.

There is a place on the North Tyne called Wark. Now try saying 'I am going to walk to Wark to work'. Absolutely hopeless: for a start Wark rhymes with Bark. This is how it should be said, assuming that you ever wish to reach Wark, and you could do a lot worse; it is certainly better than Petts Wood or Neasden.

'Ah'm Gannin tae wack tae Wark tae walk.' Now, let us try that again, all together now; that is so much better. I just hope that you divn't cowp on your heid in the witter, and droon.

I am now officially hard of hearing. For some time Mrs James has been complaining that I never listen to anything that she says. When I put this to the ENT man, he said that he had exactly the same problem with his wife, and his hearing was perfect. Anyway, it appears that twenty years of blowing the hunting horn has produced 'a classic case of noise-induced hearing loss'. I expect that you are saying that you always thought that I was a noisy brute, but although I can see your lips moving, I simply cannot hear a single word that you are saying. I am afraid that the Joint-Masters are going to have to be very kind to me.

I understand that there is a move afoot to get farmers to pay for the advice that they get from the Ministry. I wonder which side will give in first.

I am only jealous. I think that I have mentioned before that I long for hunting to be nationalized, so that I too can become a civil servant, and sink gracefully into a routine of departmental minutes, with every phrase beautifully polished, cups of tea, and gracefully referring every enquiry to another department. I wonder if I should ever have time to actually go hunting.

An interesting example of differing attitudes. I have one week of holiday in the year which I do quite look forward to, although I am always glad to get back to work. I met a nice civil servant of my acquaintance and I was telling him that I was about to be off to Spain.

'You're lucky,' he said, 'I can't see me getting a holiday this summer.'

'But I thought you chaps got good holidays?'

'Oh well, I get six weeks' leave but that's not a holiday.' There is really no answer to that.

But now enough of this frivolity. Mrs James is having one of her worthy afternoons (Fallen Post-mistresses today, I think), and my Northumbrian tutor is coming round. She says that we are going to concentrate on the Dipthong today. I do hope that I can get it in the right place this time.

Good manners, and public relations, are matters that are rightly regarded as important in the horse/hunting world. I get annoyed if I find the Blankshire field totally blocking my road when I wish to be elsewhere (quite frankly, and strictly between ourselves, elsewhere is always where you want to be as far as the Blankshire are concerned), so how much more annoyed must non-hunting people be.

Occasionally I meet strings of racehorses on the road. I know that the thoroughbred can be fairly kittle, so I always slow right down, even before the head lad starts waving me down in a peremptory manner. I will lay you a guinea to a gooseberry that no one in that string will acknowledge me. I look up at a line of sullen, wizened faces, probably with a fag stuck to the lower lip, and I wonder why I bother. Because of the horses of course.

It is a good old saying that the fish stinks from the head. Racing certainly numbers some pretty scaly citizens amongst its supporters, but surely there must be some of them with a remnant of good manners, which they could send on down the line. I did tax a trainer of my acquaintance about the ill manners of stable lads, and he said that I had to understand that they all hated cars because they upset the horses. I was still trying to work this out as he roared away in his BMW, and still am.

The main road has collapsed into a ravine, and as a result all the Edinburgh traffic has been diverted through the village and past my fields. The diversionary road is normally the sort of road where you can stop the tractor and pass the time of day with a neighbour without anybody bothering and, should you happen to stop a third party, then he too joins in the conversation.

Now we have a very different breed of punter on our little road, from huge dyspeptic lorries to thrusting Sierras with incipient ulcers. However, that is their problem, and I have no intention that they should add to mine. If I want to stop and have a word with Tommy at the bottom of the hill, as is my wont, then I shall do so. It will be a lesson in patience to those stuck behind me, and we all know that patience is a virtue, possessed by few men and no sales representatives.

There is a plus point to all this inconvenience. The bit of main road that has been closed runs through a wooded cutting which, by virtue of that fact, is normally unhuntable. I know that that cutting is filled with fat, well-fed foxes who have never seen a hound in their lives. That situation may well change.

I was interested to read that St Philomena and St Roche are the patron saints of hygiene. It had never occurred to me that there were such things, but I suppose it is no stranger than a Conservative government appointing a Minister of Drought. However redundant a Minister of Drought may be, I am all in favour of a saintly encouragement of hygiene; in fact, I think that we should all be better for a bit more saintly involvement in everyday life, and an updating of their functions. For instance, could there not be a Patron Saint of the Extraction of Useful Information from Government Departments – room for a pretty muscular ex-martyr there, I think.

What about a PS of Broadcasting? He/she could chuck the odd thunderbolt at the BBC and all those frightful sports commentators although, come to think about it, just about everybody on the BBC is frightful, with the exception of Margaret Howard and Wogan. Perhaps we could arrange for them to be martyred, and then they could take the job on.

But to return to St Philomena and St Roche. I know nothing about St Philomena, or what qualifications she had for the Hygiene Portfolio, but I was a bit surprised by St Roche. If I remember aright he was a Celtic saint, and I thought that they had all been elbowed by the Vatican.

St Sampson is my personal saint, and he has certainly been drummed out of the Brownies. I consider millstone sailing to be pretty harmless, and much to be preferred to the activities

of thoroughly tiresome saints like Augustine and Benedict with their boring fixations about righteousness. However, I fail to see that an ability to navigate a millstone prepares one to be the Patron Saint of Hygiene. I do remember that there was one Cornish saint who used to spend all his waking hours up to his neck in water, in a cave on Bodmin moor; I always thought it was St Neot, but when you think about it, with a name like that, he would not be taking much water with it, so perhaps it was St Roche after all.

I do not think that the Cornish saints ever did very much except whizz across the Irish Sea on millstones (this was before Sealink), and scupper the odd giant, with which the place was lifting in those days.

I was talking to someone the other day who had once been a footman in a lordly household. He maintained that it had been the happiest time of his life, and he failed to see how anybody could object to domestic service. I put this point to Grimling who was mucking out the collies at the time, and I thought that his reply lacked something of the old feudal spirit.

Mind you, he has been rather out of sorts ever since he read that bit I wrote about the butler and employer who got through 9000 bottles of port. I found him, the other day, trying to open the cellar lock with a bent coat-hanger and a Barclaycard (expired). I had not the heart to tell him that all the cellar contains is three bottles of Wincarnis and the skeleton of an Excise man I found nosing round that interesting little shed concealed in the rhododendrons.

I understand that it is very hard to get domestic staff these days. The full rigour of the situation was brought home to me by a snippet of conversation overheard at Peterborough Hound Show, a year or more ago. 'Poor old Johnny, I understand he is down to his last butler.' I wonder if he would like to borrow Grimling?

Everybody tells me that they can never remember the hills so wet at this time of year. We have been hunting in the back hills on foot, and in most of the places we have been, there would have been no question of riding, as there might be in a normal back end.

We were excavating in a peat hag the other day, and someone said that it would be a bad year for anyone who still depended on peats for their winter fuel because even if they had been able to dig them, there had been no sun to dry them. I am ashamed to say that this had never occurred to me. There are still a few people in this area who cut peats, but I understand that there are many more in the west of Scotland, and for them it must be a disastrous problem.

All this walking has made me like the proverbial gypsy's dog, and I lope about the place being all hearty, and telling everybody how soft they all are. However, the other day I did get stretched a bit. Between finding the fox and the peat hag mentioned above, where hounds had holed it, there were several miles of wild country. After the excavation it seemed a good time to go home, and we set off back to the meet. Just before we reached the meet, up jumped another fox and where do you suppose he went – straight back to the very same peat hag.

I can tell you that it was much farther the second time than it was the first, and I was not very hopeful, as the terriers had had enough in the cold, wet peat runners. Some of these runners are big enough for a small hound to get some way in and, just as we arrived, Wizard appeared out of the runner, proudly carrying the fox. *Then* we went home.

I wonder if you had a stag party. I think they are pretty moderate affairs, although I do not think that I have ever been to one. I suppose that this must prove that either none of my male friends is the marrying kind (Hello sailor!), or that I do not have any friends at all. You will just have to make up your own minds about that, although I suppose that, to save myself from being bombarded by a lot of GLC-subsidised gay propaganda, I should make it quite clear that that is not my particular bag.

I cannot think why I mentioned stag parties in the first place; perhaps it was because of something I heard on the Archers, where they are always doing that sort of thing.

A man in the Mart caff was telling me about a stag party he attended where the prospective sacrifice passed out. Two of the attendant guests were medical students. The sacrifice awoke to the great morning with a splitting headache and both legs in plaster. He passed his honeymoon with two 'broken' legs, and did not learn the truth until he returned home from a pretty scratchy week in Corfu. Legend has it that the bride caught up with the medical students, and they are both putting on weight, and talking with squeaky voices.

I think the most horrid stag party story I have heard of comes from Exmoor. The bridegroom-to-be had again passed out (not the same one, you understand) and the assembled company thought that it would be a terrible thing if the bride

were to mislay the groom on the honeymoon, and that he should carry some sort of identification. One of the company sold lambs to the Fatstock Marketing Corporation and just happened to have, in his pick-up, the metal ear-tags used by that august company, and the requisite pliers for inserting them in the ears of lambs for the slaughter which, in a manner of speaking, the bridegroom was. So they put one in his left ear and he spent his wedding morning at Taunton Hospital having it cut out.

The moral of all this seems to be that if you must have a stag party, stay awake.

If you take my advice you will prepare yourself for the solemn occasion as I did: with a mug of Ovaltine, an improving book, and early to bed.

The school really did not know what to do with little Brian for the school concert. He could not sing. They tried him as one of the Three Kings in the nativity play. They never did find out exactly what he did to the Archangel Gabriel behind the curtain; she was tearful but reticent about it. He was downgraded to a shepherd, but that was not a success; after all, who would have thought of a boy his age doing a thing like that with his crook? And it meant finding a new back-end for the donkey. It was obvious that Brian would have to do a solo turn, if only for the safety of the other scholars. It was the Deputy Head who had the bright idea of getting him to do some farmyard noises; after all, he was a farmer's son.

Came the great day, the concert was going the best. The choir sang like angels. The nativity play brought tears to everyone's eyes (not least the back-end of the donkey).

'Now,' said the Deputy Head, 'Brian is going to give us some everyday farmyard noises.' Applause. Brian came to the front of the stage, shuffled his feet, fixed his eyes on the roof and in a high-pitched bellow, squeaked:

'Get off that — tractor!'

There has been a big fuss around here all about the New Dads' Army. Our local paper was full of pictures of rather elderly and corpulent gentlemen presenting arquebuses. There was even an action photograph of them arresting 'infiltrators' at a local aerodrome. It was suggested that the infiltrators were played by members of the SAS. I do not wish to be unpatriotic, but if the SAS can be captured by our local paper, then I am going to join the Warsaw Pact at once.

I did belong to the TA for a short time. When I was working in the City, I joined a thing called the Honourable Artillery Company (HAC), which seemed quite a jolly thing to do. However, it was not to be; they wanted me to go to absolutely frightful places, like Larkhill, and play soldiers on hunting days, and of course that was quite out of the question.

There is one great advantage to being a member of the HAC, a full member that is, not just the subsidiary cannon fodder, which is that you cannot be arrested for poaching, unless you are caught doing it within one mile of a house where the Monarch is in residence. There is a great run of salmon at the moment; perhaps I ought to have persevered.

I did make one more stab at the TA. A friend of mine was a Militia Colonel in charge of the local lot of Donkey Wallopers. They used to spend a lot of time dashing about in long hair and armoured cars. It was rumoured that they still wore their spurs, convinced that this mechanisation nonsense was just a passing fad. They may well be right. After all, the exhaust system of a horse must be less vulnerable to heat-seeking missiles than that of a tank.

Anyway I offered this chap my services, explaining that I did not want to waste any time playing soldiers, I just wanted a nice little commission so that I could travel to London on a first-class railway voucher. What, I ask you, could be fairer than that? He got quite stuffy about it, and did a lot of heavy breathing, and turned a strange colour. He eventually said, between what I assumed to be gritted teeth, that I would only enter his regiment over his dead body. I cannot think what he got so shirty about; I was only volunteering to do my bit.

I have certainly got the right figure for the new Home Guard; I wonder if they dish out first-class rail warrants?

I suspect that a lot of you have suffered from the sickening job of stacking bales in a barn. I do not expect that you like it any more than I do. I was watching the farming programme

the other Sunday, and they had a thing about farming in East Germany.

I am not sure that life on the Old Von Donald Collective really appeals to me, but they did have one absolutely ripping idea: a bale howitzer. I understand that it is worked by compressed air. You insert the bale in the breech, press the button, and it ausfahrts from the end of the barrel and lands on top of a huge heap of bales. It is not a very tidy way of stacking bales, but I suppose that when you have the whole Prussian plain at your disposal it does not matter too much.

Even if it is a bit untidy, it must be better than Manual Labour (who is, of course, a Spanish waiter). Besides there are other benefits to be considered. I reckon that if I had one of these howitzers on top of my hill, and if I got the compressed air really jacked up, I would be able to just nicely stonk the Chairman's house; that would teach the blighter to harass me. I just hope I catch him bending over, and drop one on his nasturtium.

'Drunk as a newt': I wonder how many times you have used that interesting phrase, but has it ever occurred to you that it is grossly unfair to newts? When did you last see a drunken newt, or come to that, when did you last see any sort of newt? I do not think that I have seen one for over thirty years, nor do I suppose that they have all died of cirrhosis of the liver. The ones I remember as a child seemed to be much too inclined to an aqueous way of life to be taking much tincture on board, so why should these innocent, and rather attractive, little creatures have to carry the stigma of drunkenness?

When confronted with a problem that is both aquatic and alcoholic, the definitive experts must be Her Majesty's Navy. I rang up my friend at the Admiralty. They said that he was in a top secret conference: I said that I was M63 (southbound), and that my call would affect the whole course of the war in the North Atlantic: they put me straight through. My friend was rather shirty, saying that I had interrupted a discussion of high national importance, but at that moment I heard someone else in the room say: 'Ah but have you got Mrs Bun, the Baker's wife?' so I did not reckon that the Western Defence Machine would grind to a halt as a result of my little question.

The Admiralty had the answer. It is absolutely nothing to do with newts. Newts are exonerated; all charges dropped; discharged without a stain on their characters. It is NEUTS that are the problem. Neuts is short for Neutrals, and I gather that the phrase was coined with the Swedish Navy especially in mind.

I must say that I am greatly relieved about all those nice little newts. I intend to dig a pond one day, and I shall have no reservations about inviting some newts to come and share it with me. As to the Swedish Navy, well to be frank, I can take them or leave them, and I certainly do not want them on my pond. I did make strenuous efforts to get a Swedish *au pair* at one time, but Mrs James were agin it. In fact, the only Swedes I know are some rather jolly people who live near my mother in Spain and the last time I saw them, they were drunk as newts.

I was very proud to receive a Ned Kelly badge from my Australian friend, John Rizzo (G'day John; letter soon). John writes me fascinating letters about Australia, but sadly much of the information is such as I do not feel able to include in a family magazine; you would have enjoyed the story about the American heiress and the jackaroo.

John points out that it is a myth that the Aussies do not like the Poms, it is the *Whingeing* Poms that they do not like. Too true, mate, why do you think we sent them out there in the first place? But one must be fair. One hears a lot of static about British immigrants in Australia, but what about what they send us? As far as I can see all the Australians in this country are either dentists or social workers.

The dentists are easy to work out. They all started life in a shearing gang. When the work got a bit too much for them and they had cut off one sheep's ear too many, the Boss would say: 'You're a bloody crook shearer, mate; why don't you become a dentist in Britain?'

So away they go, take off the hat with the corks hanging round the brim, buy a white coat, collect their diploma, and the next thing that you know every town in GB is crawling with antipodean fang-snatchers. All I can say is that as dentists they are good shearers. The last one I went to see greeted me with a pair of fencing pliers in one hand and a tube of Fosters in the other. I would not have minded quite so much, but *he* intended to drink the Fosters, and add it to *my* bill.

As to the social workers; I quite see why the Australians wanted rid of them, but why did we have to get them? Surely we have quite enough home-bred meddlers and busybodies? I can only conclude that it is Australia's revenge for all those convicts that we used to ship out there. Come home, Ned Kelly, all is forgiven.

We don't have many coverts in our hunt country, but we do have one large one (7000 acres) and a sibling of some 1200 acres. The sad thing is that these were all once good hill farms, but that's another story.

The small covert has a somewhat perverse reputation. If I go there with a crowd of eager ladies and gentlemen, the foxes will run in ever-decreasing circles until dusk, when they will depart, *en masse*, over a high and unrideable hill, taking the hounds with them. Then I say to myself that this will not do; I must put in a bye-day and give the place a good rousting.

So I go there, on a horse that just needs a quiet day, with George on his motorbike, and about three hardy followers. If I do this, it is a guinea to a gooseberry that we shall spend an average of about ten minutes in the wood all day. Thus it was the other day.

I have a new horse. A very superior horse. A horse that would never have normally come my way, were it not for the fact that he was reputed to have an irremedial fault in his braking system. I bought him in July. He was at once declared to be much too good for me, and was placed under guard, in a maximum security stable.

I did once manage to sneak in and have a look at him. I was discovered, and fled, amidst a hail of buckets, dandy brushes and a particularly well-aimed pitchfork from the stud groom that scored a bull's eye and an inner. However, in November, it was decided that I could ride him, and a nice quiet woodland day would do him good, but just to jog him about, mind.

We found almost at once. We went straight away into the neighbour's country. Caught that one. Came back. Found again, and went straight out again. By the time hounds disappeared into the night (and the neighbour's country yet again), the horse was down to a walk, and the bike had clocked up fifty-nine miles, and I imagine the hounds had done at least three times that amount. All I do know is that the foxhound is a truly superb animal, and that the brakeless horse is quite one of the best that I have been privileged to ride. I wonder if I shall be allowed to ride him again.

I was thinking about the breathalyser the other day. One does think about such things from time to time. Sometimes I think about the Commissioners of Inland Revenue, or bureaucrats. I mean we all have our bad days, do we not? Anyway, there I was, thinking about the breathalyser for no apparent reason and, by the usual convoluted processes of thought, about the difficulties that had arisen when the breath-test first came into being.

I was living in Wiltshire at the time, and had been invited to a party. I did not get invited to many parties, for some reason that I have never been able to understand, so I was determined to go to this one. If I went in the car, then I would have many miles of main road to travel home. But if I went in the Land-Rover, I could come home across the drove roads on the downs, thereby missing the gendarmerie and their little plastic bags. I do not actually remember coming home, but I do remember staggering into the stable yard, the next morning, to find the staff making an interested inspection of the Land-Rover.

Somewhere, on my drive home, I had collected some 200 yards of plastic sheep-netting. It was festooned round the front of the motor and was twisted around both front wheels, neatly severing the brake-fluid pipes; further swathes of the stuff trailed out on either side. I never did discover who the fencing belonged to. The very least that I could have done would have been to buy him a drink.

I cannot leave the subject of the breathalyser without mentioning the court case in Co Louth.

A car which was seen to be behaving in an erratic manner was stopped by the Garda. When they came to look in the car, there was a man in the passenger seat, and a collie dog in the driver's seat.

When the case came to court, the defence (all this is absolutely true – I saw the press cutting) maintained that the man had never driven the car, he being already disqualified for the drink. It was the dog that was driving.

'Well, now,' said the prosecuting counsel, 'if that indeed was the case, Mr O'Rourke, then all I can say is that the dog was no great hand at driving.'

'No, Your Honour,' said the defendant, 'he's a poor driver, but then the old bitch, his mother, was just the same.' He lost his case.

Did you know that you can be Drunk In Charge Of A Horse? Well, you can. I think I am right in saying that provisions for dealing with this very serious breach of the law are enshrined within a law enacted in 1895; I understand that on being found guilty of this heinous, and disgraceful offence, the maximum penalty that you can receive is a fine of thirty shillings.

A friend of mine watches deer for a hobby. I cannot say that my inclinations run that way, but each to his own. We're all much more broadminded in our approach to these matters than we used to be. I mean, what I say is, that as long as it does not do any harm, and people enjoy it, then good luck to them, I say, well, I mean, why not?

Anyway, my friend was out early one morning, and, coming

round the corner of a ride, he came upon a fox in the act of killing a hen pheasant. In the damsel's defence a cock pheasant was giving the fox every kind of gyp, and striking at him like a fighting cock. It would have been interesting to learn the final outcome of this encounter, but the pheasant saw the *Homo sap* and fled; as did the fox, taking the hen with him.

I wonder if anyone else has had a similar experience. I had a black red gamecock that drove off a fox, but I'd never heard of a pheasant doing it.

A friend of mine – in hunt service – told me a strange story. At one time he was whipper-in to a pack in Herefordshire. They were hacking on to the meet, and their road lay between two coverts, each one field away from the road. On this morning, as they rode along, my friend noticed what appeared to be a small patch of mist on the edge of one cover, otherwise it was a bright clear morning. The mist patch suddenly thickened, and began to spin, like a tornado, and began to move quickly away from the covert towards the road.

It was slightly bigger than a man, moving fast. As soon as it began to move, the hounds and horses froze. All the hackles went up, and the horses began to sweat, but nothing would move. The swirling cloud crossed the road just in front of them, went on across the field, and disappeared into the other covert. As soon as it had disappeared, hounds and horses at once returned to normal.

My friend asked some of the locals about the phenomenon; several people had seen it, but no one could explain it. 'There are more things in Heaven and Earth, Horatio . . .'

I am slowly creeping back into the normal world after the first of the two Shepherds' Suppers that I am privileged to attend. In my experience they are unique to Northumberland, where stamina is an important factor in breeding.

The two stars of the evening were a schoolmaster who sang songs, and a man who read his own poems; all highly cultural, you see, and immensely funny. Both received the supreme modern accolade that they were 'better than the telly'; although I think that that does them scant justice. I summoned a friend of mine, a veritable Industrial Czar to come and do a toast, which he did extremely well.

At breakfast next morning, he refused food and toyed rather listlessly with a cup of tea; his conversation was minimal. At last he suggested that, as an evening, it had been unique in his experience. After another long silence during which I thought he was going to sink into his teacup, he said, rather plaintively, that he really was not accustomed to drinking quite so much.

I feel that I bear an awesome responsibility when I import these speakers from the south. The one I got last year has never been quite the same since (*see* page 88). His hair has turned grey, he walks with two sticks, and if you even mention whisky in his presence, he throws a wobbly, and large men in white coats have to come and lead him away. He is thirty-five.

If you should have the honour of being asked to speak at a Shepherds' Supper, I can only suggest that you invest in a case of whisky and do a month's intensive training. Even if you fail the course, remember – it's not the winning, it's the taking part that counts.

I tell lies. I do not tell them all the time, but every now and again, if my audience, and my mood, is right, I am guilty of flights of fancy such as regular readers of this column would find hard to contemplate.

Once I have launched myself on one of these Munchausenien anecdotes I find it very hard to get off. I was once at a dinner in London and was seated next to an American lady who suddenly asked me why I was limping. The answer to this should have been that I had recently been sat on by a horse, but without a blink I replied that it was an old war wound that played me up from time to time. From this it was only a short, but irrevocable step to my sojourn with Tito's partisans, about whom I had just finished reading a book. You will be surprised as I was that the lady took it all in, more especially when you consider that I was only born in 1940, and was capable of throwing nothing more lethal than a rattle at the time in question. As to whether the lady ever got around to looking for my shrapnel scars, I do not think that it would be fitting to discuss the matter here.

I regard my finest flight of fancy to be the movement to legalize prostitution in the City of York. I had arrived late at a luncheon because I had been having my eyes tested in York. The ladies on either side of me thought that this was a very feeble excuse, and refused to believe me, so I agreed that it was not the true story. I had, in fact, been co-opted as a lay adviser to the Diocesan Committee for the Legislation of Prostitution in York, all proceeds to the Minster Fabric Fund. The Archbishop had taken the chair; the Superintendent of Police supported the scheme; the Lord Mayor was rubbing his hands at the influx of Scandinavian tourists; the Council was going to expel all the antique dealers from one of those twee pedestrian-only streets, and fill the windows with tastefully undressed young ladies whose legs would be anything but Chippendale; the ladies would all be employed by the council, and become fully-paid-up members of NALGO.

You would not think that anyone would believe this rubbish rather than the fact that I had been having my eyes tested, but it is my experience that people will believe almost anything provided that it is told with the necessary gravitas, a fact that all successful politicians will testify to. It went down a treat, but Mrs James had been giving me her 'Just wait till I get you home' look, and after lunch she took the two ladies to one side, as a result of which neither of them spoke to me for a time.

At the moment I live in the coldest house in Northumberland, and quite the coldest house that I have ever lived in. It faces directly south-east and, in this part of the world, all the really nasty weather comes from that quarter. When the south-easter blows, our house is miserable, only two rooms are habitable, and then only in survival clothing. I have lived in cold, draughty houses all my life, shivering in six sweaters and thermal socks, and I have had enough. I have bought a bit of ground, and I am going to build a house on it; a small house, a warm house, with full insulation, double glazing and central heating. The only draught I intend to feel in the future is the one that comes out of the barrel at the Knackerman's Arms. If you want to waste your time writing to tell me that draught and draught are different, then please do; perhaps the exercise will keep you warm.

At the time of writing we are suffering from a westerly storm of what is known locally as a 'serious' wind; which means hurricane force at least. When I was feeding the ewes this morning I had to wear my cap back to front, which is a bad sign.

I then set off to go hunting. I had difficulty getting the box into top gear as we made our westing, which is a bad sign. Where the river runs beside the road, the spray was blowing across the road, which is a bad sign. Only one person turned up at the meet, and he said that it was absolute nonsense, this wind was supposed to be in the north of Scotland, not down here, and if we ignored it, it would go away. At that minute the wind tilted the box to what I considered to be a dangerously acute angle. I reckoned that the conditions had become 'serious', so I went away instead. Even with topgallants, and topsails stowed, and a double reef on the spanker, the box came home before the wind in record time. I arrived to find the roof starting to lift off, so I suppose that the house will become even colder.

Hands up those who know what a beardie collie is: as I suspected, not many of you. It is nothing like the ones you see on the box. A beardie looks like a mobile hearthrug. I do not know much about them, but the experts tell me that they are either very, very good, or they are horrid. The one I am going to tell you about was not very, very good.

Jim from the Haughs had a beardie pup. The first thing that the pup did was to grow to the size and shagginess of a Highland stirk. That was about all it did. It was not that the dog was not keen. You probably have seen a dog 'set away', it goes out wide, around one side or the other of the sheep in question, according to its handler's command – or more usually, its own inclination. After it has gone through 180 degrees and has the sheep between it and the handler, the dog will, or should, halt and await further orders with restrained and disciplined alertness.

It is not always thus, my children. It was certainly not thus with Jim's beardie. The beardie scorned the roundabout approach of his border collie cousins. He favoured a more direct method. This involved hurling himself, at maximum revs, at the sheep, scattering them to the four winds, and then proceeding in a straight line to do the same things to every other cut of sheep in the district, returning home, grinning broadly only when he had run out of steam, or sheep.

Jim took a dim view of all this, but all his steam-engine-like whistling, his enraged bellows of 'Lay down!' and 'That'll do, you!' were to no avail. Once the beardie was launched there was no way you could abort the mission.

Something had to be done. So Jim took unto himself some ten fathoms of mooring rope, tied one end round the beardie's 18.5 inch neck, took the other end in hand, and set off for the hill. It was hard work as the beardie withdrew all cooperation from the management, and dug all four huge feet in. Jim countered this move by tying his end of the cable to his stick, putting the stick across his back, and locking it in place through his elbows. So the happy pair progressed.

At last Jim felt an easing of the pull: 'He'll gan now,' he thought to himself. How right he was. The beardie had suddenly spied some sheep. By the time he passed Jim he was doing 30mph and accelerating. It is difficult to estimate the beardie's speed by the time he got to the end of his tether, but the force was such that Jim never stood a chance. With the stick trapped behind his back, he was whipped round, pulled bustle over apex, and found himself to be proceeding at great speed, backwards, and roughly horizontal, in the general direction of Bloodybush Edge.

We will now cut to where Jim has wriggled free and is lying in a peat hag, and dog, rope and stick are disappearing towards the Tweed. It is not known whether the Tweed stopped the beardie because he has never been seen again. So if you should happen to find a beardie collie complete with ten fathoms of rope, and a horn heid stick, then Jim would like the stick and the rope back. Do not ask him what you should do with the dog; he just might tell you.

'Who's a pretty boy, then?'

If my calculations are correct, this little piece should appear in the Game Management Special. McMudgeon, the keeper, and I had a frightful argument over the matter. I said that I was fed up with boring old pheasants, and that I thought parakeets and macaws would be much more interesting. I thought they would have the added advantage of being able to talk, and I suggested to McMudgeon that he should hold evening classes in the rearing pens.

I had happy visions of the more choleric type of Gun being asked if he was a pretty boy, by a Kirkcudbright-accented macaw, perched on the end of his choke barrel. Sad to relate, McMudgeon lacks my breadth of vision, and he got quite Scottish and shirty about the whole thing. You know me, anything for a quiet life, so this season I let the shoot, and McM, to The Syndicate. I have never had the happiest experiences with shooting syndicates, but I must say that these do seem a very decent lot of chaps.

They all arrive in huge black cars, and they all wear very dark glasses which does seem a bit *de trop* in a Northumbrian winter. The other interesting thing is that they always seem to carry their guns in violin cases. I mean, you would think that they would be able to afford proper gun cases, but Grimling says that it is all to do with being Italian and drinking all that wine with stove cleaner in it, and I suppose that that would affect one's behaviour.

We had rather a jolly Boxing Day, at least that is to say that about four of us did, and all the cars. The mounted field stayed back at a farm cadging drinks and chattering to such an extent that they never heard hounds find and go away, with all the concomitant trumpetings. As a result they missed most of the hunt, arriving in a steaming mass and a collective ill temper towards the (successful) conclusion. They then had the temerity to accuse me of 'slipping away with hounds'. However, I am glad to say that my lady Joint-Masters, both of whom had had the hunt, unsheathed their talons and protected my honour. Anyway the cars had a lovely day.

A high moment for me was when we thundered through the home yard. My mother is staying with us. My mother has presence, and was plucking a pheasant (you see, I am not totally prejudiced). To protect her presence she had borrowed one of my boiler suits. Mother's presence runs around, rather than up, if you see what I mean, which meant that the boiler suit contained her well, but was about 2ft too long. When she heard the hounds, she rushed out, and thus it was that rounding a corner of the yard, I came upon a 5ft mother (with presence and pearls) in a 6ft boiler suit, brandishing a semi-plucked pheasant. It is of such sights that the pleasure of rural life is composed.

This is being written just after Boxing Day. Boxing Day was a very pleasant day in this part, and I have to admit to a certain smugness as I listened to reports of torrential rain and flooding in the south and west.

I once hunted a country that had a place called Isle Abbots in it. It was a truly fitting name because even after a heavy shower the solid burghers of Isle Abbots used to have to break out the liferafts. Every time the news reported 'floods in the West Country' there would appear on the box a picture of the Isle Abbots finger-post sticking out of an inland sea. I remember remarking to Mrs James that I would lay a guinea to a gooseberry that the same hoary old picture would be appearing on 'Points West', or whatever it is called now.

With a certain sneaking sense of satisfaction I went to the back door to look at the night and have a scratch, as is my wont and, lo and behold, what did I find but a foot of merry Yuletide snow, with lots more hurrying down to join it. I wonder if any television company would like to buy a picture of an MFH sticking out of a snowdrift? It may not be much, but it must be better than the Isle Abbots finger-post.

This is the time of year when new MsFH are appointed. I think it is very difficult for a young man to be able to afford the time to learn the trade of fox hunting these days. If he cannot afford the time to learn it properly, then it would be better for him, the hounds, and Uncle Tom Cobbleigh and all if he left it alone. If you think that that is hard, then think how much harder it will be for all concerned when he makes a horlicks of it, and is thrown to the wolves.

It is probable that we shall see more professional than amateur huntsmen in the years to come, and given the difficulties of getting good amateurs that is probably a good thing.

Of course, I can blather on like this because I am approaching the end of my time hunting hounds, and I am looking forward to joining the ranks of those particularly verminous creatures, the old hunting bores. I shall start to carry a walking-stick with which I shall attract the attention of young foxhunters at parties. I shall then use it to shepherd them into a corner, far away from that pretty gel they were wasting their time with, and I shall keep them there until they faint from boredom, and the effects of that especially unpleasant brand of halitosis that all ancient foxhunters go in for (I think that you can buy it by the bottle in Jermyn Street). I am really looking forward to it.

We hunted yesterday on another day of shrieking wind. Had it not been for the fact that we had not hunted on horses this year at that time, I do not think that I would have tried. We have managed some foot days during the bad weather, but most of our subscribers think that feet are things to get unsteady on, in the four ale bar, and therefore were inclined to discount the management's efforts. They yearned for the feel of a galloping horse between their thighs. In the event, all they got was being blown half across the Cheviots, but I suppose they got some fresh air, and a good excuse to go and exercise their feet before the pubs closed. Hounds caught one fox that went all of 100 yards, and eventually found another, but we were quite unable to hunt it. Conditions had become so foul that we went home without regret.

It served to prove the correctness of the old saw that you

should 'take not out your hounds on a very wild, nor windy day', which was originally Somerville, I think.

My great uncle hunted his own pack of harriers for forty-two seasons, hunting mainly fox, but occasionally hare, in one of the rougher bits of Cornwall. On one occasion, my father and some other young bloods were staying with him to hunt in the morning. The day dawned foul and windy to the extent that Uncle Jack deemed it unfit to hunt. The young bloods, fresh from office stools, and longing for sport, raised a howl of protest. So hounds were sent on, and the party set forth packed into some species of gig with a hood on. The meet was fourteen miles away on the edge of Bodmin Moor, but with the wind behind them the little party made good time, the young men in good heart, but the Master totally silent.

At last they arrived at the howling crossroads. Uncle Jack turned the gig around, and as the full force of the Atlantic gale struck into the interior of the gig, and seemed set to lift it from the ground, he spoke for the first time since breakfast: 'Now, do you young b—s still want to go hunting?' But the young men had already repented their decision, and they had fourteen long, slow, windswept miles in which to repent it further.

January has definitely represented a 'Negative Meteorological Tranquillity Situation'. I am getting very into jargon. After all, we word processor people have to keep to the forefront of modern developments, otherwise you might think that I write my articles with a 'Portable Hand-held Communication Inscriber'. You think that I jest? Well, I am here to tell you that that neat little phrase is American speak for a pencil.

Someone told me that the reason why the Americans are so prone to this sort of awful verbosity is that the upper echelons of the American establishment are full of German extracted cousins, and German translates into English like that; things like *Obergerschenellschaftuntergerfabriken*!

The sad thing is that this sort of verbal frightfulness is catching on over here and should be resisted by all right-thinking people. The next time you get a demand for a 'Revenue Enhancement Tax Base Erosion Control', you write back and say you want a good old-fashioned 'Tax Increase' instead; I am sure your dream will come true.

'Every care must be taken to avoid running over packs of hounds which, during the hunting season, may cross the line. All railway servants are hereby enjoined to use every care consistent with a due regard being paid to the proper working of the line and trains.' It hardly needs saying that this was a GWR instruction. The GWR was indeed 'God's Wonderful Railway' to me. I have never forgotten the shock of being removed from what I regarded as my Cornish home, and dumped in suburbia, which was pretty ghastly, even in 1947.

The GWR (well, all right BR(W), as it had just become) was the way back to Cornwall, and sanity. I can never look at Platform 1 on Paddington Station without remembering the excitement of boarding the Cornish Riviera Limited (or the 'Riv' as we old Cornish hands called it), but not, of course, before a visit to the engine to see who was pulling us, and the thrill if the driver or fireman deigned to take notice of a small boy staring longingly up at the footplate.

I knew all about steam engines. In Cornwall, I had the run of the Lostwithiel–Fowey branch line, which must have been one of the most beautiful lines in the country. It was a pannier tank, push-me pull-you operation, and I spent many happy hours on the footplate, inspectors being rare birds in that part of the world, although I used to have to keep a low profile at Lostwithiel, it being on the main line. I never achieved my ambition to ride on the footplate of a King, or a Castle, and now I never will.

I have ridden on the footplate, if that is the right word, of a 125. It was very clean, quiet and frankly rather boring after a bit. The men who drove steam engines always seemed very similar to men in hunt service, they were dedicated and very proud of doing something, which, like hunting hounds, is very difficult to do well.

Some of you will remember the days when the cart stallions used to be led around the farms, all plaited and beribboned as a bridegroom should be. It has to be said that, in my experience, stallion men do sometimes tend to reflect the enthusiasm of their charges.

This fine day, the stallion man was wending his way across the open down on his way to Fagglescombe when who should he chance upon but pretty Betty from Cross Furzes. Now what pretty Betty was doing on top of the down I have not the faintest idea, nor do I think that it is any of our business. Be that as it may, it seemed a good idea to Betty and the stallion man, as it might be Bert, to sit themselves down in the shelter of a convenient patch of whins and there discuss the day, the price of sheep and, for all I know, Einstein's theory of relativity.

Bert found that to make his points more effectively he needed both hands free, and not full of stallion, as it might be Horace. There was nowhere on the open down to tie Horace so he tied him to his, Bert's, ankle. It seems that the discussion may have got rather heated and whether this upset Horace, or whether he was just impatient to get to his tryst I cannot say. What I can say is that just as Bert and Betty were reaching a crucial point in their discussion, Horace took off, and things being as they were, Bert went with him.

I do not know that there is a moral to this story except that a cart stallion tied to your ankle can cause a fundamental shift in your debating position, and badly damage your arguments.

One of the small pleasures of feeding stock in the winter is the opening of a well-made bale of hay, and receiving the sudden waft of the scents of summer preserved therein. That pleasure has been little in evidence this winter. I suppose that I am lucky to have any hay at all, but what I have got is short on summery scents and strong on dust, mould and a merry miasma of fungal spores which leave me coughing and spluttering. However, the sheep eat it without complaint, and that is what it is for. For additional energy I plaster it with stuff called pot ale syrup which looks like thick cocoa and is a by-product of whisky distilling. The ewes love it. I keep it in a monstrous tank, and get ten tons from the distillery at a time, and there's the rub. The transport people insist on sending me huge articulated 30-ton tankers which are more suited for carving up people on the motorway than for creeping up my goat track.

The first one they sent arrived on a hunting morning (this was when there was some hunting) and got himself firmly embedded in what is going to be Mrs James' kitchen but is, at present, only a glutinous mud patch. I firmly went hunting, leaving the driver scratching his head, while Tommy poked the lorry with his stick,

no doubt on the same principle as beating a horse to get it out of a bog. Anyway it was gone by the time I got back so I suppose that Tommy's goading had produced the necessary effort.

I made representations for a smaller lorry the next time: 'no problem', I was told, or to be more exact 'nae bother'.

I made a point of being absent for the next delivery, and told Mrs James to see to it. The lorry that arrived was perhaps slightly larger than the previous one, but at least it could be seen above the snow drifts.

By all accounts it was a stirring occasion, requiring the services of a squadron of four-wheel drive tractors, a mountain rescue team, and ranks of the village elders, all giving well meant, but totally useless advice. None of this availed them anything, and the driver was all for giving up and getting back to Dundee as fast as he could lay wheels to the ground. However, at this crucial moment, Mrs James rose to the occasion and bit the driver in the calf of his nearside leg. Maddened by pain and rage the driver put his foot to the floor and, with a shower of snow and dependent tractors, the juggernaut sailed to the summit, and the pot ale tank.

I do not know what will happen next time but I am having Mrs James' teeth sharpened, just in case.

I always read the hunting reports in the sporting press, with a mixture of horror and delight. There used to be one or two regular reporters, whose reports were so awful that I used to look forward to them with a sort of dreadful glee; they were compulsive reading, but how any MFH could allow his sport to be presented in this way, beats me, unless, of course, it was the MFH himself who was the perpetrator of the purple prose.

Times have changed, and people are now thankful for much smaller mercies than they were twenty years ago. When I started writing hunting reports, an old Master told me that it was bad form to write up a hunt of less than ten miles, or less than a 4-mile point. I have always stuck rigidly to this rule which is why you have not seen many hunting reports from me this season. The sad fact is that, in many hunting countries today, a 4-mile point would probably end disastrously in an 'Urban Resettlement Area', where perhaps people have not totally come to terms with their new quasi-rural environment; alternatively, a spirited gallop down the fast lane of the M243 would round off the day nicely ('a good hunt was had').

What people have not had, people do not miss. If 'a fast three-mile hunt' sends you home flushed, and glowing with excitement, just itching to get to your typewriter, then that is splendid. I am not knocking it. It is almost certainly true that the hunting that every generation enjoys is worse than the hunting enjoyed by the previous generation, but as they do not know any different, it does not matter. What matters is that hunting should go on, and that it should continue to be fun.

I have just returned from the funeral of a very famous foxhunter, Sir Alfred Goodson, Bt. I will go so far as to say that he was one of the great foxhunters of all time, and a famous breeder, not only of hounds, but also of just about everything else he turned his hand to. There was a tremendous field at the funeral, not only because he was a man much liked and respected but, I think, because people realised that with his passing, a little bit of the good, old England that we love had passed on too.

On the last occasion that I spoke to the Famous Foxhunter, I told him that it was a sin that he had never written a book, for amongst his other accomplishments, he was a marvellous raconteur. He just laughed at my suggestion, but I meant it. I think it very sad when such men take their wit and wisdom to the grave with them.

This century has produced some very great foxhunters, some of whom are still creeping about, but certain to fall off their perches in the due course of things; what a book they could write between them.

It was good to see a few bowler hats at the funeral. I have always had a soft spot for the bowler hat; I regard it as smart, comfortable and practicable. When I went to work in the City, bowler hats were still worn, but on the way out, as the length of hair increased. The only time I wear one now is for funerals, judging and Peterborough. I do not even wear them for hound exercise any more; the sad fact is that the roads have got harder, and the bowler hats have got softer, and as protective headgear they are pretty useless.

The thing that they still do well is to keep things out of the back of the neck. My father used to go and stay at a place where, after you had drunk your port, you were issued with a stick, a bowler hat, a lamp and, together with the massed terriers, the assembled company set off for the outhouses which swarmed with rats. The lights were to see the rats on the beams, the sticks to knock them off, and the hat to stop them falling down your neck.

I was a commoner once. This bald statement may lead you to suppose that Her Gracious Majesty has at last been pleased to raise me to that station in life to which I am so admirably suited in terms of birth, mental and moral pulchritude, and general superiority to the rest of you grovelling proles.

A cosy little Dukedom, you are thinking, or at least an Earldom, certainly nothing so vulgar as a Barony. However, before you put your hair in a braid, start teaching the lady wife how to curtsy while reading my articles, and apply massively for matinée tickets for my maiden speech in the Lords, let me say that I have not quite got there yet. I expect that there has been some slight administrative slip-up at the Palace; you know how these things happen. I expect they gave the chit to my friend the Black Colonel to take down to the Lord Chamberlain. Feckless young fellow that he is, he stuck the note in his halberd, stopped to dally with a lady-in-waiting on the way, forgot where he was going and why, felt like a tab, found that he had run out of papers, but found that he had a convenient piece of parchment impaled on his petard, which he could not remember what it was for anyway, so rolled a fag with it.

This, my friends, is how things happen in the corridors of power; no doubt it will all be sorted out in due course.

But I digress. What I meant was that I once had grazing rights on a common, for six sheep, if my memory is correct. I never exercised this right, but nevertheless I was embroiled in a bitter row that went to a full-blown Commons Commission. You may think that a common is a place where wombles live and that, apart from that, they exist for people to exercise their dogs on. This is far from the case. Most commons are the property of the Lord of the Manor, whoever he may be, and he can do anything he likes with that common, provided he does nothing to upset the grazing rights of those who have common rights. Common rights seem to go with the hearthstone of the house in which the commoner resides.

What this effectively means is that the owner can do anything he likes with his property except that he cannot break the sod which is the legal right of the grazier. Imagine that you are the proud possessor of 1000 acres of gorse and probably pretty derelict pasture. What would you like to do with it? I expect that you would like to grow winter wheat on it, or to develop the valuable gravel deposits that may lie underneath, or do something useful with it. Why not? The common is not used except for a few scruffy sheep, and perhaps the odd cow.

Once upon a time a property company bought just such a common: 1000 acres of virgin down on which one man in the local village exercised the rights which his family had held for a very long time. They tried to throw him off and took him through all the courts, but he won; the company was not allowed to break the turf, and to the best of my knowledge the down remains *intacta* to this day, and quite right too. I have always regarded the Enclosures Acts as pernicious:

> 'The Law will punish man or woman
> who steals a goose from off the common.
> But lets the greater felon loose,
> who steals the common from the goose.'

We sturdy commoners must stand up for our rights but, mind you, I reserve the right to change my point of view – when I become a Duke.

It is seldom that I find that I have anything in common (if you will pardon the expression) with Ms Joan Maynard, but I am pleased to say that we are *ad idem* on the matter of National Parks, or rather the matter of who runs them. The whole National Park concept is a complete nonsense. There are quite enough useless bureaucrats sending each other, and us, mountains of paper; we do not need National Parks as well. The Maynard/James complaint is that not only are the wretched things there, but that being so, why do they not employ local people?

It is possible that some of the more menial tasks may go to people who live in the Park, as it might be cleaning out all those monstrous public lavatories with which National Parks are bespattered. But there will not be any local people in the National Park Officers' Mess. The National Parks exist to provide employment for Environmental Studies graduates from redbrick universities, whom nobody else would want.

Their uniform is a beard, moleskin 'breeks' unbuckled at the knee, hairy calves, rolled down stockings, and hiking boots. Their job is to drive around in new petrol Land-Rovers, annoy farmers, and to make sure that all the public lavatories, built at vast public expense, are firmly locked from March 1 to December 31.

If we have to have National Parks they should be run by people like me. I should draw my salary and hunt three days a week. That is the way to run a National Park; I wonder if Ms Maynard would agree?

It occurs to me that I have not told you a story for some time (at this point I imagine the Editor wincing, and reaching for the office tranquillisers). This is a harmless little tale:

Len farmed at the back end of Fuzzicombe, which is the back end of nowhere.

Every year it was his custom to walk the house cow down the combe to the neighbour's bull. One day he returned from the mart in a state of high excitement. It appeared that there was a wonderful new thing called AI. He was not quite sure what it was, but it meant that he would no longer have to walk the cow down the combe. A telephone call would bring a man to the farm to do the job for them, and all the man required, to do his work, was a bucket of hot water, some soap and a towel.

Mrs Len said that well, she never did, and whatever would they think of next, she wondered.

Matters were arranged, and a day was fixed for the insemination of Buttercup, but at the last moment, an important deal over some gimmers forced Len to be absent on the big day. His parting words to Mrs Len were not to forget the soap, towel and bucket of hot water.

Came a man in a van. 'Morning, missus,' says he.

'Be you the AI man?' says she.

'Yes,' he reckoned he were.

'Well,' says Mrs Len, 'yere's the soap, yere's the towel, and yere's the hot water. The cow's in the shippen, and there's an 'ook behind the door where you can 'ang your trousers.'

This is the last time that I intend to refer to this current hunting season which I think has been the worst of my career. I cannot remember going hunting on so many really foul days. When the snow went at the end of February, we dared to hope that the season might be redeemed by some good spring hunting, as can sometimes be the case. March lulled us by starting off with some lovely weather but, even then, the Clerk of the Weather was slipping the horseshoe into the boxing glove with a view to putting a sharp one in the solar plexus.

Let me tell you about last week.

Monday was a perfect hunting day.

Came Tuesday, we found a fox at once, went away, and the fog came down.

Wednesday was a perfect hunting day.

Thursday brought gales of screaming ferocity; three trees blew across the drive, the roof blew off the collies' kennel, and a shed in the bottom field took off, and is now impersonating a wood pile in someone else's field. We did not hunt.

Friday was a perfect hunting day.

Saturday was a lovely day, if rather windy. We found a fox, went away, and another Greenland special came howling out of the North Atlantic. I have never hunted in such a wind. I am a large man, with large horses, but at one time I was being blown, with horse, sideways along the hillside. Ian tried to set off into the wind, on the bike, and it just stood still, with the drive wheel revolving. The maddening thing was that there was a screaming scent, and hounds killed a brace, in spite of the wind. By two o'clock it was positively dangerous on the hill, so we went home.

The next day we realized why the scent had been so good, as our hunter trials took place in ferocious snow squalls. That night it snowed in some tune, and, as I write, the remainder of the season is in doubt.

The building inspector came to inspect the building of the new house the other day. I was reminded of my days on the building site, in times gone by. One of the things inspectors like to inspect is whether the drains do actually run downhill.

To test this useful function, they were accustomed to put a tennis ball in one end, and send a man to wait on it coming out at the other which, if there was a fall on the drain, it was likely to do.

This sometimes produced a problem for Willie Tom's gang, with whom I worked. Some of Willie Tom's drains tended to run uphill if you see what I mean, especially if they had been put in after luncheon which tended to be a very serious meal indeed. This rather eccentric behaviour by the drains meant that the Inspector's tennis ball did not always reach its destination.

Now this would have upset the Inspector to the extent of his suggesting that the drains be relaid, a suggestion that would have been very upsetting to Willie Tom.

To avoid all these upsets and resulting unpleasantness, whomever was sent to watch the end of the drain would carry a spare tennis ball in his pocket and, after crouching over the end of the pipe for a carefully judged length of time, would leap in the air with a cry of triumph, holding aloft a tennis ball, whose appearance would be greeted with rapture by all concerned – happiness all round. This happy state of affairs continued until the Inspector started using coloured tennis balls. I call that dishonest.

Have you heard of the 'Free Boy Scheme'? This is the rather unfortunate name by which the Youth Training Scheme is known in the corridors of power. The origin of this name lies in a letter received by a well-known West Country MP, which I will take the liberty of reproducing from memory:

'When are you going to get us a free boy? My brother-in-law, he've got a free boy for his farm, my neighbour Fred down the road he've got a free boy. How ever can I keep up in farming if I can't get a free boy. I've been down to the Labour but they says that they've run out of free boys. I voted for you, so will you see about a free boy for me. If you can't get us a free boy, us'll make do with a Free Maid.'

Are you a good 'kenner'? I wish that I was, it really is a most useful gift. It is a thing that you are born with, or not, if you take my meaning. What in fact is 'kenning'? The word is most usually applied to sheep. Many shepherds know all the sheep in their charge as individuals, recognize them instantly, and have total recall.

I have the fortune to be looked after, from time to time, by a retired shepherd of repute. He comes to me at lambing time, and at other moments of stress, but the point is that he sees my ewes only intermittently whereas I see them every day.

We were leaning on a pen discussing a ewe that I was a little worried about. That, he said, was the 'ard bitch that we had in a pen to herself at the end of the passage'. He was talking about lambing time a year ago. I remember that we had a ewe separated, but I am blessed if I could remember which it was. He had retained her picture in his head all that time; nor is that an isolated example of his skill: he 'kens' sheep well.

It is the same with hounds. Some people seem to be able to recall, not only every hound that they have hunted, but also every hound that they have seen at a show. I simply do not have that gift. I can learn a pack of hounds fairly quickly if I see them every day, but if I go back through my kennel book there are an awful lot of names to which I can no longer fit faces and yet at the time I loved them dearly.

My mind does not work that way, and yet it is not that I have a bad memory. I can quote you chunks of prose and poetry that I first learnt over thirty years ago, and, if you give me too much to drink and Mrs James cannot head me off in time, I will sing all night songs that I learnt by ear and have never forgotten.

So perhaps I am a good kenner in my ways. It is just that, like all my meagre skills, what I ken is totally useless, and has no practical application at all; the story of my life, really.

I do not know much about the Swedes, and Mrs James is resolutely determined that I shall not add to the sum total of my knowledge by getting in a Swedish *au pair*, but I suppose that if I were asked to give a thumbnail sketch of this most fascinating of peoples, I would say that they were gloomy, randy and pretty useless at dealing with Russian submarines.

Now I have been forced to see the Swedish nation in a totally new light. Their latest scientific breakthrough just could have the biggest influence on the behaviour of mankind since the invention of the sliced loaf.

A lady Swede obtained her doctorate at Stockholm University by producing a 300-page thesis that proved that a pedestrian in a hurry moved his, or her, legs faster than one who was not. I wonder if you are as shocked and stunned as I was by this mind-blowing revelation. There is no doubt that the lady doctor of whatever she is now a doctor of has made a major contribution to the sum of human happiness, and the Swedish nation must be rightly proud of her; almost as proud as we were when our Arts Council gave a grant to two men who walked about with a plank on their shoulders claiming to be a living sculpture.

If I came behind them with a ruddy gert stick, do you suppose that their legs would move faster? If I meet them I will try it, and publish the results of my scientific experiment in this column.

6

It is the seventh day of April, and it is blowing a blizzard yet again.

Mrs James has run the metal clip from the end of a halter shank right through her hand, and is looking like a bit of advanced tapestry work.

Mrs James's dog (The Fraggle) has found, rolled on and gorged off, something very dead and indescribably foul.

The collies are bickering.

The Patterdale is going about with stiff legs and raised hackles, itching to give somebody, anybody, a right seeing to.

I had two cervical prolapses this morning: well not me personally, you understand, I leave that sort of thing to the ewes, which never fail to rise to the occasion.

Master James has a friend staying, and they are occupying their time by testing an intergalactic-mega-gargleblaster, which proceeding leaves a lot to be desired for those seeking a reposeful session with the muse.

I have got the influenza. It is snowing some more.

All together now: eyes down for a quick burst of 'Ours is not a happy household'.

However, let me not burden you with my problems, as I am sure you have many of your own. The 7.45 late again was it? Points failure at Carshalton I should not wonder. And as for that traffic jam on the Western Avenue, well I mean, the whole thing has become quite definitely intolerable.

By the time you read this, all these separate little bits of misery will just be unhappy memories, and we shall be skipping, you and I, through verdant fields, amidst the fragrance of the spring flowers, while lambs gambol, and birdies twitter among the brown ale cans and other litter. Then shall we loiter upon some mossy bank, make a daisy chain (not in my fields you won't; there is no moss, and, at three tons of lime to the acre, no blasted daisies either). Then maybe we shall feel once more the rise of the sap, and burn each other with glances full of a meaning as old as mankind; and at that moment along will come another blizzard.

The problem is that it appears to mean exactly the opposite at different ends of the country. If you were to say to someone in Brighton or Bristol that you doubted that it was going to rain today, this would indicate to them that you reckoned that the weather would stay fine. In Yorkshire and places north, doubt appears to mean exactly the opposite. 'I doubt it will rain today' means you are quite certain you should be taking your mackintosh with you. I found this very confusing at first, and I wonder why it should be. Perhaps doubt in the original suggested a degree of indecision. This indecision has swung to the negative in the south and to the positive in the north, and I feel sure that there is something very profound to be read into that.

I have never been minkhunting. I should like to go, but there are no hounds near here. We all got very excited one year because an MMH, as I assume them to be titled, wrote to ask about bringing his hounds up here. I canvassed some of the local landowners who were enthusiastic, as mink are becoming an increasing nuisance in the area. But since then not a squeak of a minkhound have we had; always supposing that that is what minkhounds do.

When young, I thought that it would be the thing to hunt foxes with your hounds in the winter and otters in the summer: much more fun than hound exercise. I have no doubt that 1027 people will write to correct me, but I think that the last pack of hounds that performed such a dual role were the Carmarthenshire.

The best otterhunting that I can remember was with the Hawkstone in the late 1950s and early 1960s with the redoubtable Capt Wallace.

Otterhunting was always best on a big water where hounds had to swim. River Boards, pollution and mink have done for the otters and otterhunting. There is nothing to do in the summer now, except work.

Visiting cards were a bit before my time, but if I remember aright the procedure was somewhat as follows. You rolled up at the drum you proposed to visit and rang the bell, or better still got your man to ring the bell. The door would then be opened by a suave servitor who would receive the card and disappear with it into the nether regions 'to ascertain whether the mistress was at home'.

The fact that you had already clocked the mistress peeking

round the curtains in her boudoir was neither here nor there, and had no bearing on the fact that her man came back to tell your man that she was 'not at home'. You knew she was at home, she knew that you knew, but you had called and left your card, the politenesses had been observed, the King Emperor was on the throne, and all was well with the world. All very civilized, and quite unlike today where you just barge in and find the mistress degunging the Aga.

A young couple married and set up house. They were a bit strapped for cash and suave servitors were out of the question. The best they could do was a girl from the back of beyond, as a maid of all work; a nice girl, a willing girl, but not versed in the mysteries of 'service'. With great patience the young wife coached her in the arts of waiting at table and, of course, in the business of answering the door, taking the visitors' cards and asking them politely to wait while she went to see if 'the mistress was at home'. Came the day that the sound of an approaching dogcart was heard: the first caller.

The young couple fled to the stairs, to watch and listen. The maid clumped her way to the door. There was a murmur of conversation from the front door, then a bellow from the maid: 'I've got their tickets, Missus, do I let 'em in now?'

Thank goodness for the faithful Grimling; his front door manner may not always be quite what one would desire, although I have managed to persuade him to stick his cigarette behind his ear when he is addressing the quality. But, as he says, no bailiff has ever got through any door that he has the answering of, and with a talent like that, one can be a little lenient, don't you agree?

I have two pieces of simply fascinating information for you.

The first is that the City of Birmingham takes in 80,000,000 gallons of fresh water every day, and puts out 90,000,000 gallons of sewage. Now does that not just blow your mind? Is not that just the most fascinating bit of information that you have read for a very long time? But just pause for a moment, and study the figures again; you will see that they do not balance, and the only sense that I can make out of it is that the solid burghers of Birmingham must get through 10,000,000 gallons of beer every day. I do not know what the adult population of 'Britain's Second City' is, but their per capita daily ale consumption must be truly ferocious. I wonder if A. Spokesman would like to comment?

The other bit of fascinating information is that the Gentry no longer exist, and that is official.

I know this because I happened to go on a course and we had to consider the Socio-Economic grades that are used by officialdom to split our society into manageable chunks.

These grades run from A to E. I will not bore you with all the details but, if you take my advice, you will avoid being in group E; everybody's got their boot into them.

The top of the dunghill is Group A. This comprises 'airline pilots, bank managers, solicitors, dentists, etc.' That is it, the pinnacle, the penthouse suite. I felt that this matter required some further investigation. In spite of being in a sort of semi-coma that had been induced by a very moderate luncheon, I raised my hand.

The female *sturmfuehrer* who was conducting the session asked what my query might be.

'What group,' I asked, 'do the Gentry come in?' For a long moment she examined me, and obviously found little to gladden her heart.

'They no longer exist,' she said curtly, and turned back to the blackboard.

So there you are. If there is anyone out there who thought himself a Gentleman, then I have got news for you, Squire, you no longer exist; and that is official.

The lambing has finished. Haggard, unshaven, and bloodshot of the eye, I am returning once more to normal life, and full nights of sleep with my clothes off. I was deeply grateful for my new shed, which has been a great success, as the weather has continued to be atrocious.

I have not dared to speak to any of my friends on the hills yet; I fear that a lot of them will have fared badly. I did see one hill shepherd who had 2ft snow drifts to struggle through.

'Oh! to be in England-Now that April's there'; all very fine, but Browning had the sense to write those lines in Italy. Let me return the compliment.

'Blow, blow ye icy winds and rain,
next lambing time, I'm off to Spain.'

This brings us neatly to the Holiday which is once again rearing its ugly head, and once again Mrs James and I are off to the land of Rioja, paella and siesta, more or less in that order.

So fed up are we both with being treated like mindless lumps of vegetable matter by the local airline that we have decided to go by train.

A day in London to carouse with my fellow MsFH, and to buy the Annual Shirt.

A day in Paris and what I get there will depend on how closely I am guarded by Mme James, and then on the Talgo to jolly España, to a rapturous welcome from the burgeoning James Fan Club on the Costa Blanca.

I would prefer all hound shows to be divorced from accompanying agricultural shows. If I want to look at heavy horses, or double-sprocketed combine-harvesters, then I will bestir myself to go to a show to see them. If I go to a hound show I go to look at hounds, and have a crack with the few remaining foxhunters who are prepared to speak to me. I do not want to sit for four hours in a queue of traffic with a load of barley barons, or anyone else for that matter. Nor do I then

want a hike from the car park to the hound show that requires a compass, a sleeping-bag, and rations for a week. In the course of this walk I am persecuted by long-haired show jumpers, mown down by police Land-Rovers, and pursued by fat, perspiring men with electronic megaphones. I can do without all this. I want to be able to drive up to the show, park and wander, unhindered, among fellow enthusiasts, without so much as a hint of a Dagenham Girl Piper.

Mrs James and I are off to Dublin this year too. I have never been to the Dublin Show, but I have been asked to attend in the official capacity. I am sure that it is a mistake, but I hope that they do not realize it until I have got there.

I do not think that I have been to Dublin for nearly thirty years, and the last time I was there I got totally hog-snarling. However, I am sure that both Dublin and I have changed for the better, I shouldn't wonder.

I was listening to a lady rabbiting on the wireless. She was in a high state of excitement because her particular part of north London 'had managed to maintain a village atmosphere'; now that is a particularly ghastly thought, and only someone who has never lived in a village would think a village atmosphere to be admirable, or desirable. We had the same thing throughout the miners' strike, with trendy sociologists wittering on about 'tightly-knit communities' as though they were a second Eden: tightly-knit communities are hell.

I have only lived in a village once, and I would never live in another, unless I owned it.

The townsman regards village life as the epitome of rural bliss, with apple-cheeked rustics, in embroidered smock frocks, rushing from one thatched cottage to another, feeding each other elderflower wine and calf's foot jelly – when they can spare the time from dancing round the maypole, that is.

That is not how life works in a tightly-knit community. For a start, everybody knows everybody else's business, and what they do not know, they invent. All TKCs are hotbeds of gossip, tittle tattle, and rumour mongering, usually malicious, because as Captain Bob and Rupert Murdoch know, good news is boring.

If you want to hear a really professional hatchet job going down on someone's character, just hang about the old village pump.

Feuds are another happy aspect of TKCs. It is quite normal for half the village to refuse to speak to the other half. The feuds are usually tribal and the cause, if it were ever known, has long been lost in the mists of folklore and time. Each successive generation will fall to with enthusiasm to stoke the fires of rancour and bitterness.

Most villages have a pecking order. Upward mobility is not encouraged, and anyone trying to climb the ladder is likely to get his fingers firmly stepped on by the person on the next rung up.

Of course, there are some admirable things about village life: old people are unlikely to be allowed to starve to death, and children are unlikely to be abused without detection, but there is a price to pay, and that is feather pecking, and a complete lack of privacy: perhaps that is what the lady on the wireless is striving to achieve in her north London suburb. I wish her joy. Anyway, here comes Fred up from the village, I must break off and get up to date on all the latest gossip.

I rather regret not having gone for a soldier when I was a young man; who knows, I might now be a Field Marshal instead of a peasant farmer and scribbler.

I feel sure that ability, intelligence and all sorts of other goodies are what are required of the potential officer in today's highly trained professional army; they probably always were, but I do remember a school friend of mine going to be interviewed by the Colonel of the Hot and Heavy Hussars. The interview was brief, and went like this.

'D'yer hunt?'

The friend had been cubhunting once, had fallen off, and declined to repeat the performance.

'Ever ride point-to-point?'

An absolute negative.

'D'yer play polo?'

The friend suggested, as tactfully as he could, that the idea appalled him.

The Colonel stared at him for a long moment, and said, 'Well, yer don't seem to have much military nous. Ever thought of the RAF?'

The closest that, at that stage, I had come to the military was compulsory enlistment in the Combined Cadet Force. I was flogged by the head of the house for having a dirty rifle, and generally did not enjoy it greatly. I expect that fellow sufferers will remember those awful Field Days where one had to crawl about desolate bits of heath in southern England, discharging blank rounds from one's Crimean muzzle-loader.

Every so often an officer would leap out of a fuzz bush and scream: 'Bang! Bang! You're dead.' You then sat about and ate your sandwiches, until someone blew a whistle and told you to go home.

It did not always work like that.

A certain very aristocratic cadet was trolling along across the heathery wastes, when he was ambushed by an umpire. 'Bang! Bang! You're dead.' Without so much as a flicker of recognition the cadet continued his stroll while the umpire snapped frantically at his heels, 'banging', and 'you're deading' in ever more frenzied tones.

At last the cadet could stand these ill-mannered importunities no longer, and confronting his frothing adversary, he murmured 'Wumble, wumble, I'm a tank,' and continued serenely on his way.

People keep telling me that I ought to fish; they say that I would enjoy it. I did try it, and I am not sure that I have the patience for it, and I am pretty sure that I do not have the time, nor the money, at the moment. It seems to me that I might enjoy fishing a decent bit of water, where there was a sporting chance that I might catch something, but you will be surprised to hear that no one has yet offered me a rod on the Tweed.

The only sort of fishing that I might possibly be able to afford is the sort where there are no fish. There are those who would seem to be quite happy flogging a fishless piece of water all day, and wondering whether they should change their Purple Sprouting Spinner for a Pittsburgh Stogie, or whatever. They get peace, tranquillity and away from the wife, more or less in that order.

All I would get is my line tangled in a sheep, and bad tempered. Also I can never manage all those funny little flies, and those awful fiddly knots; I need a man to do that for me. I do not think I shall be fishing this summer, therefore.

I have an antipodean problem. I have a Kelpie. It is at this point that some of you clever herberts out there are going to say things like: 'Well, don't pick it then,' or 'keep taking the tablets', so we will have a brief pause to get all that out of the way . . . Better now? Good.

A Kelpie is an Australian sheepdog. It is small, reddish-brown, smooth-coated, with prick ears. It barks; St Australasius, how it does bark. But it don't half shift sheep and, no doubt, in time as it gets older and wiser, I shall get it to shift them the same way as I want them to go. Its enthusiasm is boundless, and its stamina is bottomless. It is a thoroughly nice dog, and its only faults are those of inexperience and youthful over-enthusiasm; all faults, that is, except one.

It piddles on Patterdales. My Patterdale terrier is just a convenient height. I am a sentimental man. I have always had a personal terrier, and one of that terrier's duties is to come and sit on my lap and to be affectionate to the boss (who gets precious little from anywhere else) while he says stupid things to it in a silly voice. The fact that affection, Patterdale-style, consists of sinking its fangs through to the bone if I so much as move a muscle, is neither here nor there; that I can put up with. What I find much harder to put up with is a Patterdale who has received a massive overdose of antipodean pollution.

I do not know if you have been trying to telephone me lately, but if you have, you will have been having problems getting through. The reason for this is that we have a portable telephone which is immensely useful until your wife drops it in the khazi, whereupon it tends to sulk, and withdraw all co-operation from the management, pretty much as Mrs James has been doing since I felt it incumbent upon me to point out to her that it was a bloody silly thing to do.

The other day I got lost in Newcastle's Eldon Square Shopping Centre, if you really want to know. The Eldon Square Shopping Centre is a classic example of the evil that men do remaining years after they have gone, and I think that those responsible for perpetrating such horrors on the British public, should be condemned to wander for ever through endless corridors of burgerbars, boutiques and shops selling mechanical aids to marital fulfilment.

I really thought that I was never going to get out of the wretched place, and it took a couple of large gins at the club to restore me to something like normality.

I was doubly sore because I do not normally get lost. I am blessed with an especially acute bump of locality and direction. Not everyone is so blessed. Mrs James has trouble finding her way from the Aga to the sink. In fact we had our first row over direction. When we were first married we lived where

Mrs James had lived and hunted all her life. We set off cubhunting one foggy morning, and arrived simultaneously at the centre of Pinkney Park and a disagreement.

'To the right, I think, my dove,' said I.

'Not so, my hero,' said she. 'We must, I fear, go left'.

'I must disagree with you, Jewel in my Crown,' (this is me again). 'I respectfully submit that the meet is to the right.' At this Mrs James got on her high horse, which is not a very easy thing for her to do; perhaps it would be more apt to say that she reared up like a bit of fried bread, and gave me the whole 'I've hunted here for twenty-eight seasons' bit, which would have been all right except that I was right all the time. If there is one thing no wife can stand very much of it is a husband who is right all the time, and so I am occasionally reduced to getting lost on purpose, just to save my marriage.

Here we are back from the holiday. My dears, you simply cannot imagine what an exhausting time we had, such fun, and *screams* of laughter; all too, too amusing.

But first, the annual trip to London. I did not buy a shirt this year, after all. I still had last year's on, and Mrs James tells me that you can actually wash them and wear them again. Is it not quite amazing the things they think of these days? I mean, I have always worn my shirts until they start to disintegrate, then I just put the new one on over the top. This year I bought three new bow ties instead. So look out around the shows, you are in for a treat.

And so to Spain.

I had left all the travel arrangements to Mrs James; after all that is the sort of thing that one's people are for. I am determined to try to be fair about the outcome of her efforts to transport, in comfort, a large and choleric MFH across Europe, but as the MFH in question, I may perhaps be forgiven if a somewhat subjective whingeing note occasionally surfaces.

We spent the night in Dover.

It was a splendid hotel with rooms overlooking the East Kent bus depot. I would like to take this opportunity to praise the zeal of the excellent maintenance department of the East Kent Motor Traction Co. So keen are the fitters on producing their vehicles to the high standards required by the solid-citizens of E. Kent that they sit up all night banging, hammering and revving engines, yea even unto 0300 hours.

Mrs James decided on the hovercraft. I was rather looking forward to a bit of the Yo Ho Ho on the ferry, and had even packed my telescope and parrot, the better to stride the poop deck; however, this innocent pleasure was to be denied me.

A hovercraft is noisy, smelly and hot, and it was packed with schoolchildren who were noisy, smelly and hot. Any view that I might have had out of the tiny window was totally obscured by spray. In the nicest way possible I was able to spend the time pointing out to Mrs James the drawbacks of her chosen means of transport.

At Boulogne we had an hour to wait for the Paris train, or so Mrs James assured me, as we watched it pull away in front of our eyes. I really think that she might have realized that our European partners have not yet discovered the blessings that flow from having the same time as we do in Britain.

Paris was wet.

The Talgo trains are the pride of Spanish railways. I looked at the substantial French rolling stock, and thought that they promised a certain roomy comfort. The shock when I finally came face to face with the Barcelona Talgo was considerable. The luxury carriages are the size, and shape, of the rolling stock on the Bakerloo line. The Spaniards are small, and neat, and can be packaged away neatly on meagre shelf space. I am not, and cannot.

I will draw a veil over the night, except to say that it provided me with ample opportunity to discuss with Mrs James the efficacy of the arrangements so far.

The plan the next morning was to catch the midday Talgo to Valencia, which entailed some wait at Barcelona, which is apparently the largest railway station in Europe. However, Mrs James discovered an earlier train which called itself a Transvia. I asked the nice girl at the information desk whether there were restaurant facilities on the train: she regretted not. I thought that her smile was a little sinister. When I saw the Transvia I realized why.

The late Percy French wrote a song about a local train in the west of Ireland; it had a line that went: 'It all depended whether the ould engine houlds together, and it might, now Michael, so it might.' This is the theme song of the Transvia, and so curious are the Spaniards to find out when the inevitable is going to happen that they pack on like sardines, so as to be there when the final disintegration takes place. The thought of dissolution worries the driver so he drives very slowly, with his hand on the air horn, presumably so the emergency services can monitor his progress. Every so often he appears to be overcome by despair and, stopping the train in the middle of nowhere, he takes out his keys and with much shouting and gesticulating leaves the train and stomps off to a trackside telephone where he has long and animated conversations, presumably with his confessor. He then stands brooding in the middle of the track, scratching himself in a rather intimate fashion, waiting, I suppose, for Divine Guidance.

I do not usually talk much to Mrs James in public, but as there was no other English speaker on the train, my choice was somewhat limited, and it gave us a jolly good chance to review the travel arrangements so far which had possibly not quite come up to the high standards of care and comfort that a man in my position needs.

Everything flowers in the end. We had a week of lovely weather, good food, and just the occasional glass of wine, and we flew home.

On occasion, some of the bright-eyed, idealistic, young people, who are the new MsFH settling into their posts, seek Old James's advice. If they do not, then I back them into a corner, subdue them with my halitosis, and give it to them anyway. I always try to impress upon them the importance of a good first impression.

I will give you two examples of getting off on the wrong foot.

A keen hunting farmer of my acquaintance thought that he would take himself to the kennels, and meet the new Master. He was informed by the staff that the new MFH was in his cottage, so he went and banged on the door. The door was opened by a person in a plastic mackintosh, fishnet stockings, and not much else. My friend was a little surprised by this, but rallied, and said that he had come to see the new Master.

'I am the new Master,' said the vision.

The other story is about when the Hunt Chairman gave a large dinner party for the new Master. The party waited in growing despair for his arrival and eventually sat down without him.

Came a telephone call. It was the new Master. He was very sorry but he was (a) in London (b) drunk (c) in bed with a naughty woman, and (d) on all these accounts not coming to dinner.

I offer no moral judgments, although I remain to be convinced that transvestites make the best Masters. I merely say that if you want to do things, do not tell your Chairman about it, and whatever you do, do not frighten your farmers.

What of the new house? So people keep asking me, and I am most grateful for their concern. It shapes well, my dears, and we hope to move in in August. This means a lot of turning out and a certain amount of ruthlessness has been necessary. Mrs James and I both suffer from the 'it might come in useful one day' syndrome, as a result of which nothing gets thrown away, and we have been elbow deep in years of accumulated clutter: old bits of clothing, old photographs, old letters, and piles of totally useless bric-à-brac that 'might come . . .', but of course, they never have, and never will, and they are for the chop.

Some favourite bits of furniture are going too. The selection caused us not a little heart-searching, but the fact is that we are moving from a quart pot to a pint pot, and the contents have to be adjusted accordingly. We have become quite hardened, Mrs James and I, and I am filling boxes of stuff for her to carry out to the growing pile of disposable junk; but then, as I like to point out to her, I knew that she would come in useful one day.

I am always somewhat depressed by my total inability to master matters mechanical. I flatter myself that I am quite a good hound man, and stockman. I am a rotten horseman, but I am a worse mechanic. Machinery is a closed book to me. My only remedy for a malfunctioning machine is to clout it with a lump hammer, and you would be surprised how often this seems to solve the problem. If the problem is more complicated then I send for a mechanic. I do not like doing this, not only because they are expensive, but because they are always sixteen, covered equally in acne and oil, and they always regard me with ill-concealed contempt.

They arrive and walk round the machine shaking their heads, and sucking their teeth. I suspect them of a suppressed desire to call me 'Grandad', but my bulk, and the lump hammer swinging in my hand, just about prevents that. They suck their teeth again, scratch their crutch vigorously, whip an enormous screwdriver from behind a grease-encrusted ear, and make some minute adjustment somewhere in its lower intestines.

'Try it now, squire,' and I do, and of course it goes like a dream.

'What was the problem?' A withering stare.

'Yer intersprocketed flange innit.' Stupid question, of course; any fool, except me, would have known that, and five seconds and £30 (plus VAT) later they are off down the drive – and how close they came to taking my lump hammer with them, somewhere in the back of the skull.

There was a time in my life when I tried desperately to get to university. My father was a rowing blue, and to him university meant Oxford or, if he took a deep breath, held his nose and swallowed hard, Cambridge. To their eternal shame neither Oxford, nor Cambridge, showed the slightest enthusiasm for gathering me to their academic bosom. To be fair to them, I showed neither academic nor social brilliance, nor could my father afford to pay for the refacing of a set of cloisters, which is how one of my schoolmates achieved a degree in history, in spite of being a youth of quite numbing stupidity.

My father was then reluctantly forced to accept the existence of such places as Reading and Durham. I suppose it is possible that these admirable seats of learning failed to realize the plum that was being dangled, so temptingly, in front of them. Their attitude was that when it came to youthful, acne-ridden Jameses they could take them or leave them, and on balance they preferred to do the latter.

In the end it came down to the stark fact that there were only three seats of learning prepared to take academic no-hopers like myself. One was in France, and I cannot even remember the name of it, one was Trinity College Dublin, and the other was Cirencester.

France was out. Father and I both agreed that Abroad was

Bloody. I was very keen on TCD because I like the Irish, and I believe that the best Irish is drunk in Dublin, and the best Irish are drunk in Dublin, and I wanted to tag along. However Father decreed that Ireland was both Abroad and Bloody.

This left Cirencester.

I knew a lot of people at the Royal Agricultural College at that time, and it seemed to me that they spent all their time, when they were not hunting, being sick at dances. It is quite possible that I am being immensely unfair to the administrators of the college, but that was how the place seemed to operate at that time, and I was all for it. I am sad to say that the college appeared to Father in the same light, and he were agin it. Even Cirencester was denied me, which has been a matter of lasting regret to me. If I have appeared to be somewhat unfair to the RAC, let me point out that that generation of Cirencester students produced, not only some of the foremost of our present day agriculturalists but also some of the ablest current MsFH; on both counts, it must have had a lot to recommend it.

I know Cirencester has changed a lot. I knew it was changing when a friend of mine, a mature student, a man of highly-polished shoes and brilliantly-burnished manners, was forced to walk out of an examination hall at the RAC because he

could not stand the oppressive odour of bare, sweaty feet which were the current student fashion.

I knew it had changed a lot more when I saw three Cirencester students on the box. I could not see their feet, but they had things about doing it in wellies all over their chests, and they were talking, very knowledgeably, about 'Cash Flow' and 'Gross Margins'; then I knew things had changed. In my day, a gross margin would have been a strip that you left round the edge of the winter corn for the hunt to ride on.

I believe that this article may well appear in the Game Fair number. As I write I glance at a full page in the current *ST*, entitled 'Meet the Team'. What a splendid bunch of red-blooded Britons, and with what pulchritude the Editor staffs the office, and what a thrill I should get if only I could persuade Amanda Taylor to handle my advertising. However, it will not have escaped your notice that one name, and one picture is conspicuous by its absence, to whit *mine*. I hasten to add that I have no desire to go to the Game Fair. I did go once and it left the most dreadful emotional scars.

What I want is the odd freebie. It is impossible to pick up the *Shooting Times* without finding someone writing about the marvellous trip they have been on, the marvellous gun they tried (supplied free), the charm and efficiency of all on Outer Mongolia Airlines (free tickets, and unlimited Siberian Champagne), and the immense comfort of the Strength through Joy Hotel and Bicycle Repair Shop, in Ulan Bator (free food, rooms, and unspecified comradely benefits). The ostensible reason for all this subsidized frolicking is a serious expedition undertaken, in conditions of great hardship, to establish whether the Outer Mongolian Sandgrouse, on receiving a charge of No 6 up its backside, falls to the ground headfirst, or not, as the case may be. The results of this fascinating enquiry will be discussed gravely, and at length, and will probably gum up the correspondence column for a twelve month.

This is the ostensible reason, but I know, and so do you,

that it is just a jolly junket that the writer has conned someone else into paying for. So what, you say, jolly nice work if you can get it, and that is exactly the point, I, Arthur Wilberforce James, am not getting it, and what is more I am not getting any free trips, free waterproof jackets to test, or free knives to sever my thumb with, or anything, and I think it is all jolly unfair, and a swizz and rotten, and I shall probably spend the rest of the evening sucking my thumb and sulking. I am quite certain that *Shooting Times* must be required reading for any self-respecting merchant prince, or captain of industry, all seeking some nice venal journalist who will write nice things about their products. I am that man, and my copy will be just as fair, objective and unbiased as you care to pay to make it.

The next two weeks promise to be anything but dull. The Mobile Dipper has been very busy this year. In the last three weeks we dipped some 25,000 sheep, and the period still has time to run.

I have been getting lambs away, which is very early for me.

I am a staunch monarchist but I did feel a bit miffed when they held The Wedding on the same day as Wooler Mart. It meant that we were quite unable to take our places in the Abbey (you no doubt noticed the two empty seats somewhere to port of where Prince William was picking his nose), and Mrs James was left at home with a pile of sandwiches, a mountain of Kleenex and the telly. I was really quite sharp with the Lord Chamberlain about it; I felt that things should have been arranged better, and I have to say that feelings ran quite high in the Mart canteen. However, I wish the happy couple well. She looks a good, big girl and should carry twins, I reckon.

I love the autumn hunting on the hills, and I would be hardly human if the thought of my lowland brethren still exercising between fields of green and soggy corn did not add a little piquancy to the occasion. This will be my twenty-first season carrying the horn, and also my last as huntsman, so I am hoping even more than usual for an open and good-scenting season. I wish the same to all when that green and soggy corn gets cut.

I have just been reading an interesting article in a magazine for country landowners (have to get that bit in for the rest of you proles) about communications on shooting days which can be a bit of a problem apparently.

I remember observing a shooting party which included a man with a black labrador which he had attached to his person by ten fathoms of strong cord for reasons that quickly became apparent. When the action started, the dog registered its enthusiams by galloping in ever-decreasing circles, with the result that man, dog, stick and gun finished up rolling on the ground in a sort of cat's cradle whilst the pheasants whizzed overhead.

I did not think that man had any problem in communicating his thoughts, which were colourful and imaginative. I knew that it was important to break your gun to avoid accidents out shooting, but until that moment I did not realize that you had to do it over a dog. It just shows how much I have to learn.

There were some interesting little sketches in this article aforementioned, which demonstrated some of the Shooting Signals. For instance, if you raise your gun over your head, but keep your hat on, this means: 'Bring the Powder and Shot'.

If you put your hat on the end of the fowling piece and raise both above your head, this means: 'Luncheon' and richly deserved, after all that heavy lifting, I should not wonder.

If you keep your hat on but raise both hands above your head, this will indicate: 'Dog wanted'. I suppose it could also be used to indicate: 'Well, I did not know that he was the local MFH when I shot the fox.'

It seems to me that the signal system could be usefully adapted for hunting. Let me offer one or two possible suggestions.

If at the end of a hunt you see the Master dismount, throw his cap on the ground, and start jumping on it, this will almost certainly signal: 'The Chairman has forgotten to stop his earth again.'

If the Master puts his head down an earth, and displays a large expanse of enbreeched backside to the field, this will indicate: 'It is a nasty cold, bad scenting day; I am nicely in the shelter down here, I am going to have a howk.'

Some signals would require a more positive reaction. For instance, if you see the Master running across a ploughed field and waving his arms in the air, he will be signalling: 'I have fallen off, and lost my horse; I want yours.' You should take immediate steps to deal with this situation and, if you have any sense, they will be fast – and in the opposite direction.

My Irish Affairs correspondent tells a tale of a certain local council in the Republic, a member of which went on holiday to Venice and came back full of enthusiasm for gondolas. He suggested that it would be a great idea if the council purchased one as a fine addition to the local lake. The Council thought that this was a grand idea, and one member, who had not been to Venice, suggested that they should buy two, one male, and one female, so that nature might take its course; a sort of Irish Shallow Draft, I suppose.

The female of the species never ceases to amaze and mystify me. It had been decided that it was time for my Patterdale bitch to have a litter. It was thought a splendid idea, and a high-powered committee was formed to arrange the nuptials. The Borders were scoured from end to end to find an eligible bridegroom with all the necessary attributes to match.

At last the prince was found, and all that was necessary was for Jessica to cooperate. Jess, being what she is, steadfastly refused to come into use. She only comes in once a year anyway, and then only if she feels like it; and she did not.

Nature cannot be defied indefinitely, no matter how small, black, and nasty you are, and eventually the necessary situation was achieved, and Jess went away to stay with the prince for a week. Every opportunity was offered her, and every luxury lavished on her to encourage courtship, but she would have none of it.

She arrived home in disgrace, grinning all over her face.

Within five minutes of being home she got herself lined by one of the collies.

There the matter rests, and so does my case regarding the perversity of the female mind.

A friend of mine went to stay at one of the few remaining houses where your case gets unpacked for you. If you come and stay with me, Grimling will of course unpack your case, but just make sure that the bottle of whisky that you are going to give me is not in there, because neither of us will see it again.

My friend had some dirty socks etc wrapped up in a piece of a well-known tabloid newspaper, in the bottom of his case. These were removed. The next morning he found his smalls, newly washed and ironed, and laid out on the bed; beside them, also neatly ironed, was the bit of tabloid newspaper.

It is nice to know that standards are still maintained.

To be fair to Grimling, he always returns the empty bottle.

To Dublin. My dears, such excitement: such packing and repacking of suitcases; such agonizing over what to take and what to leave behind. However, after much drama, I did relent and agree to take Mrs James, and a fine August morning found us at Edinburgh Aerodrome, watching the sleek jets roll down the runway, and waiting for our sleek plane to appear.

At last a furtive-looking man sidled up and, speaking out of the corner of his mouth, asked if 'Youse were for Dublin?' 'Yes, yes' we said eagerly. He directed us through several flights of stairs and corridors, through the canteen kitchens, and out past the bicycle sheds, and there was the plane. It was not a sleek jet. It was what is known as a wind-up job.

This plane had several interesting features. I noted the open cockpit where the pilot, in a Biggles' helmet, kept giving us reassuring thumbs-up signals. The co-pilot, immaculate in bowler hat and shiny gaiters, had a halter on the plane's head, and I am sure that he comes in very handy for opening the gates on the runways. I had a peek in the little compartment at the back, and there was a boiler and two little men in green top hats were stoking it furiously with peats. They must have worked jolly hard because they got us to Dublin five minutes early – although, to be fair, there was a following wind and the Captain was able to set the spinnaker.

It is stupid to go back to a place after thirty years, and expect to find it unchanged. I have affectionate memories of Dublin in the late fifties, and I found the Dublin of the eighties rather depressing, and sleazy to be absolutely frank, and desperately expensive. An American said that it was becoming like Naples, but without the sun. Even the Guinness failed to be as I remembered.

On the credit side, the developers have not had it all their own way, and sizeable chunks of Georgian Dublin have been saved for a posterity which is perhaps more concerned at having to pay 16 punts for a bottle of whisky. By the way, you will find that the Irish are more than happy to accept sterling, and if they sometimes forget that the punt is only worth about 89p, that is only because they are a little overexcited by the pleasure of having you in their country. You will find taxi-drivers are particularly susceptible to this form of hospitable hysteria.

I had never been to the Show before, or the RDS as it is known. The R stands for Royal, and you might be forgiven for pondering on this in a Republic which is not as full of Anglophiles as it might be. The answer is that there was a vote on it, and an overwhelming majority voted to retain the 'Royal'; make of that what you will.

Whatever, it is a truly splendid set up, and very well organized.

It is only of recent years that the hound show has been held as part of the horse show. It used to be held at Clonmel, and there are those who feel that it might benefit from a return.

The hounds are shown on a stage in a ring where bloodstock is sold. The result is that the seats for the spectacular are quite the best of any hound show anywhere. After all, the sort of seat at most hound shows, which we all moan about but do nothing about, certainly would not do for your genuine Bedouin from whom you wish to extract a mass of petro-dollars.

A lot of hounds take exception to the somewhat exposed situation and refuse to take an active part in the proceedings, and I cannot altogether blame them. I felt for the hunt staffs who did not find it easy to get the best out of their charges.

The Senior Judge was a Very Senior Foxhunter indeed, and I only hope that he enjoyed judging with me, as much as I enjoyed judging with him, but I suppose that is not very likely.

It may or may not be of interest to note that the previous occupants of our stage had been the Bolshoi Ballet. I regret to say that this gave rise to some rather unflattering comparisons from some of the rougher elements amongst the spectators. I felt compelled to suggest to the Senior Judge that we too should put on a display of terpsichorean expertise should our performance be in any danger of flagging. He looked at me and asked if I had the 'Elephant's Tango' in mind for my own contribution, which I thought was a bit uncalled for, so I sulked, but later cheered myself up by trying to imagine him in a tutu.

I never learn. Once again I have been guilty of hubris, and once again my pride has been humbled. I recently had had a self-satisfied snigger about how I would be hunting while all the rest of you would still be exercising. There is an old Arab proverb that says that life is like a cucumber: just when you think that you have it firmly in your grasp, you find it stuck ... well, somewhere pretty unpleasant, I can assure you. What all this is leading up to is that, two days ago (and two days before our puppy show) with hunting only a week off, hounds started coughing, and all our plans are knackered. Instead of the puppy show, I am working in the office, and am feeling sick as a parrot.

I have been involved with hounds for some thirty seasons, and it is the first time that I have ever been stopped with lurgy in the kennels. When I was a young man, I do not remember ever hearing about coughs, sniffles, sneazles and all the other things which now seem to lay hounds low every year in some part of the country. Where have they all come from? And why do they not stay there?

I think the answer to the last question is not difficult to find. We are all much too mobile these days. We go all over the country to hound shows. Beagles go frolicking and festing all over the shop. Gundogs bring their owners from all parts of the realm to seek the sole remaining grouse that is rumoured to be holed up somewhere in the north of England (I understand that the Scots are experimenting with haggis this year). There was a little local sheep dog trial the other day, and I was told that there were dogs there from Cornwall, Shropshire and Sussex. All in all, it is small wonder that coveys of viruses (Viri? Vira? or even Vera, come to that) are winging enthusiastically all over the country. I just wish that they had not all selected my kennels to drop on.

I suppose that there cannot be many more shopping days to Christmas, and you will soon be thinking about the Christmas cake. Spare a thought for Sarah, and her Christmas cake. Sarah always made a marvellous cake, rich and fruity and lots of marchpane (*archaic variation of marzipan, Ed.*) and icing. On the top there was always a little hunting scene with little lead figures that were treasured and brought out every year.

The cake was made and decorated, and put on the kitchen table: exit Sarah, stage left. Enter, stage right, Blankshire Smellwell, puppy of that ilk. Exit, centre stage, one Christmas cake.

We will not dwell on the scene of domestic disharmony that followed; suffice it to say that there was a crisis. The disappearance of the cake was a problem that could be remedied, but the little lead figures were irreplaceable.

There was only one thing to be done, and it called for patience, vigilance, and intense monitoring of *all* Smellwell's movements.

Patience was rewarded, and it came to pass that a new cake was made complete with a hunting scene with little lead figures.

Another slice anyone?

My neighbour does not know the Facts of Life. Most hunts in this area operate a Ewe Scheme. If you have never met one, it looks like this. The hunt buys a ewe and takes it to a farmer, who then runs it with his own flock, lambs it, and in the fullness of time the lambs go to the Mart, and the proceeds are credited to the hunt. It is a valuable source of income.

The neighbour keeps a ewe for us, and one for the neighbouring hunt. I should say, in all fairness, that apart from this latter blemish, he is a man of the highest possible moral character, and is kind to widows and orphans (in case his wife should read this, I hasten to add that of course I am only talking about very, very old widows).

I met this excellent man in a state of some distress. He claimed that both his hunt sheep had fallen off their perch within forty-eight hours of each other. I had to take him gently by the lapels of his coat, and point out to him that, although he was an experienced flockmaster, he had no concept of the Facts of Life, or Death, in so far as they concern hunt sheep.

Hunt sheep are truly marvellous creatures: they never get ill or lame, they never fail to rear at least a pair of lambs, and they certainly have never been known to die; that would be quite impossible.

My neighbour had not until then grasped these essential facts, but as I gently shook him up and down, he began to see that he might have been mistaken, and a well-placed knee finally clinched the matter for him. So, the Hunt Ewes live on, and my friend is in full possession of the Facts of Life. I find that most people are responsive to rational argument, and a little gentle persuasion.

We are in the new house. We have been in residence, in a wasteland of packing cases, for ten days. In that time we have had three different lots of people to stay. To get this fact in perspective, I should point out that this represents an increase of 300% when compared with the whole of the previous twelve months. People were reluctant to come and stay in the old house (a) because it was difficult to find; (b) because we never bothered to carpet the spare room, and (c) because I would not want to stay with me, so why should anybody else.

However, the new house is so convenient for travellers to and from Scotland, and so carpeted, that they come in spite of me. Anyway they all just ignore me, and Mrs James sends me out to grumble in the sheep shed.

One of the things that intrigues me, on my rare visits to the Great Wen, is the number of four-wheel drive vehicles that one sees stuck in the traffic. They are always bristling with bull bars, and acned with spotlights, but one look at the trim and the tyres is enough to realize that these unfortunate machines have never seen a muddy track in their lives, and have probably never known the thrill of being in four-wheel drive, except that is for the Range Rovers with the smoked windows. Who buys these things and why? In Northumberland you are very well advised to have some form of four-wheel drive capacity, but do you really need a jeep to ascend Hay Hill? Is Hampstead so frequently cut off by storms that you need a Daihatsu to get back to civilization? The whole thing is a piece of roaring snobbery. Even if you work at the BBC, have a wife who wears pink dungarees, and get agoraphobia in Holland Park, you still like to give the impression that you cannot wait for 12 August so you can drop everything and hurry away to your moor.

And the Lock's hunting cap that sits permanently on the back seat of the Range Rover has never been worn. However, eventually it can be turned upside down and made into a hanging flower pot.

But I suppose that it is all a pretty harmless little conceit, which indicates Urban Man's yearning for his rural roots. In fact, it is much better if he acts out his role in the town; it is when he comes out of the town and tries to make the country conform to his rural idyll that things come unstuck.

Anyway I am no one to talk about little conceits. When I go to London I always carry a most professional looking briefcase. Its contents? a packet of sandwiches, a flask of whisky, my book, pipes and tobacco. Do not tell anybody. It is just that I have this suppressed urge to be a merchant banker.

We have started hunting. The cough is behind us. Sport has been good. I am knackered.

We start hunting in our rougher country, right out. Allow me to put this in perspective for you, before some unhappy creature from Sussex writes to me to say that their hunt has a covert that is at least a mile from any road.

The farm where we met on the first morning has a drive four miles long, and its road end is ten miles from anything that might possibly resemble a main road. Behind the farm there is a considerable flap of peat hags, which you might just negotiate on a horse after a very dry summer, but the way things have been this year, it is a tackety boot job.

We had a busy first morning, about seven hours, with hounds disappearing over the top of the Cheviot, and then coming in again, for which relief we were very grateful. The morning finished with a howk in a peat hag, from which we all emerged plastered from apex to bustle.

I am writing this after our second morning, in a different bit of country, not as high as the first bit – I mean, nothing much over 1,400ft, but much steeper. We found a good strong litter, and hounds hunted continuously for some four hours. All the action took place across the grain of the country, if you follow me, with hounds always disappearing over the next ridge into the next valley. This meant sliding down 600ft, with the prospect of climbing up 700ft at one in three.

It goes without saying that as one gained the summit, one met hounds coming back, and if only one had had the nerve, and patience, to stay where one was in the first place, one would now have been ideally placed. But, of course, if one did that, there was always the risk that they might have gone right out and one would have seen them no more for quite some time.

So one turned round, and slid down 700ft, and climbed up 600ft of one in two shale, and as one gained the summit, one met hounds coming back, and, of course, if only one had had . . . But I suspect that you will have got the picture, and that is why I am knackered.

A man told me that a lot of the men who used to herd in that bit of country just described lived to be a hundred, because of the strength and purity of the air, and the beneficial effects of continuously climbing those hills. I believe him. It would be quite impossible to work in those hills and be unhealthy; you would either be very healthy, or dead. I do not think that there would be much room for a compromise.

I think that there can be no doubt about the beneficial effects of walking. Among the older generation of hill shepherds you will see no fat men. They are lean, spare and hard as teak. Their deceptively slow, slack-kneed walk is a snare and a delusion to lesser mortals. Lesser mortals say to themselves, 'I will burn up that shambling old fool. He does not look as though he will make the top of the hill anyway.' The lesser mortal will do well if he stays upsides of the shambling old fool for five minutes. The shambling old fool will draw effortlessly away, and just as effortlessly will disappear over the crest, whilst the lesser mortal stops yet again to try and pump some air into his bursting lungs and persuade his legs that they cannot seize up just yet.

Mind you, the younger men carry a bit more flesh. The farm bike, on which they are wizard performers over the most hideous ground, has taken a lot of sweat out of their work, but they would still out-walk most of us.

There is no doubt then that exercise trims away the excess flesh. This being so, why are the modern beaglers so fat?

I went to a show the other day, where a well-known pack of beagles was parading, and the thing that impressed me, apart from the excellent turn out, and the splendid condition of the hounds, was the globular state of the hunt staff. I wish that I could get bums like that on my sheep. I should have thought that beaglers, by and large, taking into account the amount of exercise I assume them to be taking, should look like the proverbial gypsy's dog, but I have to say that the word that springs to mind is 'pudgy'.

There is a character in the *Memoirs of a Foxhunting Man* who says something to the effect that 'whisky is all right for foxhunting, but you need beer for beagling'; could it be that many beaglers – a body of people for whom I have the greatest possible admiration – are interpreting this man's advice too literally, and maybe too liberally?

I pose this fascinating question purely in the interests of the people concerned. I would be failing in my duty as a responsible journalist were I to do otherwise. But, knowing how little people like having good done to them, I fully expect some pretty stroppy letters on the subject.

I have no doubt that I shall be accused of pontificating on matters that I wot not of. If this should be the case, let me say that I have before me a picture of myself when young, and a whipper-in to a famous pack of beagles, in which I look like two yards of pump water, as they say in Cornwall; or did when there were any Cornish still living there.

So there, I ran, and I was thin. Let modern beaglers follow my excellent example, instead of merely running to fat.

At the aforementioned show a little group of us MsFH were leaning on the ringside, chewing the fat, and indulging in a little quiet character-assassination, as tends to happen when two or three foxhunters are gathered together. Someone wondered what the correct collective noun for a group of Masters might be, and indeed I think that there is some little scope for entertainment here, so let us consider the matter.

I seem to remember that my suggestion at the time was a 'lust' of Masters, knowing the somewhat priapic tendencies of most Masters given half a chance, and inattention on the part of the wife. This was rather shrilly rejected by the Lady Master present who pointed out that she was not that sort of girl. So we shall obviously have to find something different.

What about an 'expletive' of male Masters, and a 'shrill', a 'screech', or a 'tantrum' of Lady Masters.

A 'waffle' of Hunt Chairmen must answer that problem rather neatly.

What can one say about Hunt Secretaries? Well, quite a lot, in my experience. What about a 'quibble', a 'misprint', or a 'doyoumindtakingthecapsbecauseI'mofftoKenyaforthreeweeks'?

I have just thought of a smashing one for girl grooms, but as I don't want a pitchfork through my ear next time I go to the stables, I'll pass on that one. A 'howk' of terriermen, or even a 'nearlyuptothedog'; a 'knacker' of kennelmen; a 'moan' of subscribers; a 'blockage' of car followers.

I am rather partial to a glass of champagne, provided that someone else is providing it. But I have noticed a disturbing trend lately which seems to suggest that champagne is not for drinking, it is for shaking up and spraying at television cameras. What an appalling waste this is, but every time some berk wins something he gets a magnum of bubbly which he promptly sprays over everything in sight.

I used to comfort myself after a fashion by telling myself

that no doubt the organisers would have plenty more around that the chap could enjoy at his leisure, after all the excitement had died down. Now the truth is out. I watched a thing on the box where the crew of a New Zealand yacht won something, sprayed everybody with champagne, and then settled down to drink cans of beer. Can there be any hope for civilization?

I am going to offer a service to the organisers of all so-called sporting events. I will attend with my stirrup pump and spray anybody they want. I do not want paying. I will settle for the champagne.

Today is the first of October. It is a lovely day. I hope that the weather continues in its present mellow mood.

September was a month of almost unbelievable splendour in this part of the world. Of course, I am terribly sorry that you had all that nasty rain, drizzle and fog in Sussex, and other such quite unheard of places, but then I do not suppose that anyone of any consequence lives there anyway, so it does not matter very much.

Now I must tell you that yesterday we had quite the hottest day's hunting that I think I can ever remember; in fact I consider that it was about the hottest day we have had all year, and Newcastle was the hottest place in Britain which is not a state of grace that it achieves all that often.

My dear, we just panted out on the hill. There was a breeze, but positively Saharan, and there was no scent, and of course some By Our Lady fool came up and told me that it was a lovely day for riding about, and then whizzed away, before I could get the first Oath out of the little case in my pocket where I always carry them. There is a charming little man on the *Socialist Worker* who makes them up for me, and very reasonably too.

One thing in particular cheered me up in the evening. Mother telephoned from Spain to say that they had had three days of torrential rain and thunderstorms, and wasn't it terrible, and she supposed that it was much worse with us, wasn't it? No, I said, prodding the punkah wallah to work harder, it was not, but I understood that it was ghastly in Sussex. Well, said Mother, what do you expect in a place like that, and surely no one important lived there anyway . . .

What you are going to read now has absolutely nothing to do with country sports or pursuits. It is also a very, very sad story, but it is full of human interest and sociological import, and so I feel it behoves me to explode it. It is a true story, and concerns 'The Batman of —'. Blank is what the tabloids would refer to as a 'sleepy market town', and may, or may not, be on the Scottish borders.

In Blank there is a row of terraced houses inhabited by Caring People, to the extent that seeing ten milk bottles piling up on the step of No. —, and knowing that the occupants, Mr and Mrs Blank, were in residence, they started hammering on the door.

There was no reply.

The gendarmerie were summoned. They hammered on the door in an official sort of way.

There was no reply.

In spite of local advice, the sergeant did not think it necessary to summon the SAS. He felt that the Blank Police could break down the doors with the best of them.

So they did. There was no one about. Then from upstairs, an undeniable muffled groan. So up the stairs, at the double, went Scotland's finest.

In the bedroom they found a lady wearing only a gag, and handcuffs, with which she was firmly attached to the bed. Then from the wardrobe, more muffled groans. The wardrobe was forced open to reveal a man in a Batman suit firmly wedged inside. It was quite natural that the constabulary should be more than a little nervous about this somewhat bizarre situation, as all of you out there are, I feel sure.

The explanation was quite simple. It was the husband's custom, having firmly secured his wife, to don his Caped Crusader outfit and climb to the top of the wardrobe, with a view to taking a flying leap and thus adding a little piquancy to what, I suppose, might otherwise become a somewhat humdrum and run of the mill operation. However, on this occasion, at the crucial moment, the roof of the wardrobe gave way, and Batman disappeared into the depths, and became totally jammed there. And there the matter rested, as you might say, for some two days.

I must say that I have found the whole matter thought provoking: anyone out there want to buy a part-worn Batman outfit? I think that I may well take up beagling instead.

A week of frenetic activity: two rather jolly days to finish the cubhunting, including a rather decent hound hunt out into the neighbour's country, which is always good for discipline. Then a quick dash home, a flying change, and off to speak at a shepherds' supper, so I was not that early to bed. The following night it was the hunt ball, and the next morning the opening meet. All in all, a fairish test of stamina, especially as some work had to be squeezed in as well.

We had the hunt ball at our only castle, and it was rather sad because the castle has been sold, and there will be no more dances there. It was a truly splendid evening, but marred for me by the prospect of having to be on the ball the morning after the ball (if you see what I mean); it prevented me braiding up my hair and hitting the place a crack. It was quite obvious that no one else felt themselves to be under any similar restraint, and I have to tell you that there were some pretty sorry sights at the meet on the following morning. There were indeed some notable absentees, and many who felt that their horses were just not quite fit enough for the opening meet, or something.

I have to admit that, left to my own desires, I would never go ball dancing, but it is expected that I should attend my own hunt ball. I am not quite certain as to why people should insist on this; it hardly seems as though my presence rouses the punters to paroxysms of joy, or encourages them to even greater heights of terpsichorean excess. Everybody seems to spend the evening telling me what a miserable blighter I am. I cannot see any necessity to get dressed up just to go out and be told that. I can stay at home and have Mrs James tell me that, in comfort.

The problem is that I am a kindly, easy-going chap; I will hurt no man's feeling intentionally. What then should a man do when sitting at a pub table, longing to go home and watch Postman Pat, but whom is nevertheless confronted with

the fact that lined up on the table before him are eight tots of Grouse whisky which kind people have bought for him.

Over-indulgence can have some strange results. A friend of mine catches eels. He came home with a batch and not wanting to deal with them at that moment he put them in the bath; well, you would, would you not? He then had his tea, lit his pipe, and dozed off in front of the fire. He was awakened by hammering on the door which opened to reveal Fred and a bottle of whisky. The bottle was more or less full, and so was Fred.

A glass or two was taken, after which Fred shambled to his feet muttering about seeing a man about a dog, and disappeared into the bathroom. There came a sort of shriek, and Fred reappeared apparently in some sort of convulsion and beckoned the friend. Together they stood silently watching the writhing mass in the bath. At last Fred managed to speak: 'What's that in the bath?' The friend, who has a mean streak, inspected the bath carefully, and said, 'It looks like a spider to me.' 'A spider? Nothing else?' 'No.' 'I see,' said Fred, and very carefully and very uprightly he marched out into the night. He left the whisky behind, and the eels were delicious smoked. If you can extract a moral from this story then I wish you well.

I wish to protest to those who advertise sporting and outdoor clothing and equipment. I am not objecting to the stuff that they advertise on the whole, although we may return to that in a minute. My point is that they are employing totally the wrong sort of chap for the job of modelling their wares.

I am not arguing about the crumpet you see filling the sweaters with lambs gambolling all over their . . . well, the undulating parts; I never argue about crumpet, and come to that I never get the chance to do much else with it either! However, that is not the point at issue, as the actress said to the bishop. What we are on about is your actual male model.

I have a selection of glossy magazine advertisements spread out before me on the desk, advertising variously wax-proofed cotton garments, hunting clothes, and the most ghastly jacket ensemble that I have ever had the misfortune to see. In fact, I am going to withdraw my criticism of the model wearing the putative shooting suit. It is quite obvious that only someone like that could possibly wear a suit like that, but where and for what purpose he would wear it defeats me. Unless, that is, he had got a walk-on part in Emmerdale Farm. Perhaps he is the one who drives the Land-Rover that has never had mud on it, and chucks bales of hay (with the band uncut) to the sheep in June.

Let us consider our other two outdoor types. It is quite obvious that the most rugged feat that they have ever performed is to climb the stairs at Earls Court underground station. I am quite certain that they are the most charming people, pillars of the community, subscribers to a myriad of worthy causes, but as examples of Outdoor Man they are a total frost, and it is time that this fact was brought to the attention of the manufacturers concerned.

What these manufacturing chappies want is the right sort of model; someone who will give rural authenticity to their products. It is no use them draping their products on these herring-gutted weaklings with 30in chests; what sort of image is that? What these manufacturer chappies want is real Outdoor Man; someone about 6ft tall, with a 50in chest, no neck to speak of, and the sort of face that can only be authentically produced by forty-five years of exposure to wind, weather and whisky; oh yes, and he really ought to have a moustache, a proper one, not one that looks like a scrubbing brush after the hound puppies have borrowed it.

Now here is a strange coincidence. I have just realized that the above description fits me rather well. Who would have thought it? So there it is – I feel duty bound to offer my body to the greater glory of British manufacturing.

The other night whilst in the bath, I was thinking about false teeth – and why not? Not that I have false teeth, Praise Be. I am blessed with a very sound set of choppers that come through my tail female line, my great-grandmother having handed in her dinner pail, at ninety-one, with a full set of her own teeth.

What had set me off on this particular line of thought was the unfortunate thing that happened to the mother. You may remember that the mother went off to live in Spain; well, you may have forgotten, but I am quite sure that the wretched

Spaniards have not. The mother is not too struck by the Spanish dental service, so the last time she was over, she shimmied into Newcastle and had herself fitted with some high-class fangs. Whilst drowsing through the heat of an Iberian afternoon she decided to remove them for no very clear reason that I have been able to establish. When she awoke from her 'secure hour', she found them gone. There now follows a considerable saga of search and rescue, which I will miss out, as some of you out there with nervous dispositions might find some of it rather harrowing.

The upshot of it all is, or was, that the teeth had been borrowed by the dachshund belonging to the solid Swedish couple who live close by, which presented the teeth proudly to its owners who, in turn, re-presented them to the mother who then rang me up to get her a Christmas appointment with the Fang-Snatcher for repairs and maintenance. In the meantime, I fear that the poor old soul may be reduced to a liquid diet. Oh dear.

Anyway, that is why I was thinking about false teeth, whilst I was in the bath. I thought of a lovely man, now deceased, with whom I have drunk a lot of claret whilst we talked about everything from Shakespeare and Surtees, via foxes and pheasants, to the Thirty-Nine Articles. It was his wont when greatly exercised over some tricky point to take his teeth out and put them on the table in front of him. I was always rather worried that if I argued with him too much, the teeth would run across the table and savage me.

It is impossible to blow a hunting horn without teeth. A one-time neighbouring huntsman to me suffered badly from ill-fitting teeth which he hated wearing. He used to compromise by slapping them in his mouth when he wanted to blow his horn, and sticking them in his pocket when he did not.

I was out with those hounds one day. They found in a neat gorse covert on a hill. Tremendous cry, holloa, the twanging of the gone away, we all rammed our hats down and thundered round the corner of the covert . . . The only way out of the field was a stuggy gateway through which seventy South Devon cows went to and from their milking every day. Hopping about on foot in the gateway, with mud up to his garter straps, was the huntsman. With infinite sadness we watched hounds disappear over the horizon, and then addressed ourselves to the much more interesting task of seeking Fred's teeth in 100 square feet of rich Devon mud.

The onward march of science does not always leave a trail of unmixed blessings. Does everything have to be wrapped in the sort of plastic that requires a pair of bolt cutters to open it? And if we did not have television, then we would not feel bound to watch the crud that the broadcasting people produce on our screens. It is certainly true that there are on/off buttons on televisions, and I use mine instantly at the first whiff of a politician. At least television has demonstrated to even the weakest intellect what an unsavoury bunch they are; right, left and centre. However, there are two scientific developments that I welcome without reserve; to whit, the bleeper and the ATV.

Probably most readers will know what a bleeper is. I think it was originally designed for use on ferrets, but people were quick to realise its application to terrier work.

There is a collar that goes on the dog which carries a tiny transmitter, which sends out a continuous signal (always provided that you have remembered to put the batteries in). The hand-held receiver bleeps, and by moving it about and varying the volume, you can not only locate the exact subterranean spot where the dog is but also how deep it is, up to a maximum of 15ft.

When I think of the hours I must have spent over the past thirty years lying flat on my ear on cold, soggy ground listening for the terrier, and the subsequent hours of often wasted excavations, then I do applaud the bleeper.

Mind you, they do require a bit of practice to handle

accurately, and to dig to the instructions of an unskilled operator can be a somewhat frustrating business for you, and a chastening one for him. It is probably best to practise a bit at home before you take to the field with your bleeper. Do what a man I know did: get your butler to take the collar under the dining-room table, and crawl about with it; you will soon get the hang of it.

The other invention which meets with approval is the ATV (all-terrain vehicle). In case you have never met one, they are small, three- or four-wheeled tractors, with huge bulbous wheels. They have many agricultural applications, being able to travel over sodden fields without leaving a mark. I use mine round the sheep, but it gets bored with that and likes nothing better than a bit of hunting; sharpens it up no end, in fact.

An ATV will go almost anywhere that its operator is capable of taking it, which means that some go more anywhere than others do. In certain types of country they are, in fact, better than a horse because they do not sink where a horse might (they do not float, by the way). They will stand patiently for hours at a hole, or outside a public house (or so people tell me), and no one has the vapours should they not return to base in good time. They will carry collies, terriers, bags of feed, bags of lunch, spades, and the odd nubile nymph should the coast be clear; all in all they are extremely useful, and I am only sorry that they did not come into my life twenty years ago: just think of all the extra bye days there could have been.

An example of the appliance of science failing to bring unallayed happiness occurs to me. This sad little story was told by my cosmopolitan brother, who knows all about this sort of thing.

Cable TV is apparently the coming thing, and it came to a block of flats in Turin (the one in Italy, just in case there is one in Dorset, or Kirkcudbrightshire; where is Kirkcudbrightshire, anyway?). There was living in the flats a young (mixed) couple who became aware that the other inmates of the flats were beginning to give them what used to be call 'old fashioned looks'; they, and no doubt you, wondered why. The reason was as follows: the couple took great pleasure in each other's company. They liked to have friends to visit them too, and then they all used to take great pleasure in each other's company.

It was the wont of the young couple to film these lively get-togethers on their video camera. When they were on their own they could put their feet up, pour a glass of grappa, and turn on the video to watch their own personal match of the day. The only snag to all this was that, thanks to some quirk of the cable system, the video appeared not only on their own screen, but also on all the other screens in the block, and you know what neighbours are: me, I am all for it; it must be better than EastEnders.

I am being worn down by people continually asking me why I am giving up hunting hounds, so I will beg the indulgence of our sainted Editor and use the pages of his magazine for a personal statement.

The return of my horn to its place of retirement on the mantelpiece has more to it than meets the eye, as you all rightly supposed. However, the real reason is not for general disclosure, and I must ask you all to treat what I am about to tell you in the strictest possible confidence: the fact is that I am being put out to stud. For some time the Masters of Foxhounds Association has been concerned about the declining physical and cerebral standards of modern MsFH. You have only to look about you to see some of the utterly appalling specimens who currently struggle feebly with the dreadful burdens of Mastership.

The powers that be felt that something must be done. A highly emotional meeting was held at the Cavalry Club, and it was decided to arrest the decline by instituting an intensive breeding programme.

The trouble has stemmed from a modern obsession with

pace, and the result is that most modern Masters conform to the Super Ferret Standard. Go to any hound show in the summer, and you will see any amount of these unfortunate creatures – weedy, flashy, herring-gutted, all teeth and Adam's apple. Pace, yes, I grant you that they have pace; they will be up to the bar, and through three gins and tonics while most of us are still unchaining our wallets from our braces. But where's your stamina? That's what I want to know; where's your staying power? Are these human whippets up to the strain of drinking a bottle of port after dinner, and still fulfilling the arduous nocturnal duties that are expected of a Master?

The sad fact is that they quite simply cannot stand up to the pressure. They pack up hunting at 2.30pm, and still flake out, face down in the soup. It must be obvious that such a situation cannot be allowed to continue. So the MFHA instituted a countrywide search for the best type of old-fashioned MFH, a solid, well-built type, with irreproachable stamina points, prominent bloodshot eyes, a vermilion face, good

heavy jowls, and very likely a moustache, with bits of last night's casserole in it.

Of course, there was little doubt as to where they could find all these excellent qualities encapsulated, if not neatly, then certainly fully, and so I was approached. I am not a man to shirk my duty, however arduous and, on occasion, distasteful that duty may be. However, so onerous and physically taxing do those duties promise to be, that I felt that they should be incompatible with hunting hounds. I am, after all, only human.

Now to my gamefowl – silver duckwings. I was given a cock and two hens when I first became an MFH. The lady who gave them to me said that no hunt kennel looks right without a gamecock about the place, and I think that she was right. They certainly seem to thrive around the flesh house. I have had them ever since. I never take any trouble with them; they just run wild about the place, eating, fighting, and . . . well, you know. They do a lot of that, and as a result there are a lot of broods every summer. Again, I do not bother with them, and nature takes its course; some survive, and some feed the foxes. The population usually settles down at about twenty, and if there are too many cocks, well, gamecock is monstrous good eating.

We had one the other night, by mistake. He was rather a nice young cock that I was thinking of taking on the permanent staff. I had come into the yard with a big round bale on the transporter, on the back of the tractor. It seemed like a good moment for a cup of what Mrs James loosely refers to as coffee, so I stopped and, being a conscientious tractor driver, I lowered the hydraulics. It seems that the young cock must have come strutting underneath, just in time to receive 300kg of hay. He was very tasty, but rather flat.

There is always a senior cock, and over the years I have had some very good ones. I always name them after friends of mine, and if you think that a lot of my friends are arrogant, priapic, male chauvinists, then it is not for me to tell you the way that you should think. Let us return to the story.

A friend came to visit who was, and is, an authority on gamefowl, and he much admired the reigning cock of that time. We used to correspond regularly on hound related matters, and he never failed to enquire after the gamecock. We did not meet for some years. When I saw him again, I was standing outside the beer tent at Honiton Hound Show surrounded by admirers (you would surely expect nothing else?), when up comes your man:

'Arthur,' he says, 'how's that lovely cock of yours these days?' Right, just you try explaining that one to the sort of people you get in the beer tent at Honiton Hound Show.

It is not far from Honiton to Exmoor, a place of which I have many fond memories, and a place where I have always thought that I would not have minded living if the lines had fallen unto me in different ways. One day I shall go staghunting again, but I do not know when. It is a long way to drive for someone of settled habits. It would be an even longer way to walk and that was what made me think of a man I once met on Exmoor.

His grandfather, or maybe even his great grandfather, had been the man who brought the first flock of Scottish blackface sheep to Exmoor. Grandfather walked the whole way: sheep, dogs, family, everything. It took them a year. It was a pretty remarkable feat, and I wish I had taken more notice of the details of the story. I suppose that they came straight down the M6.

Last Saturday we had what is known locally as 'a big day at the hounds'. We had a sharp, but inconclusive, hunt in the morning. Then at about 1pm we found another fox.

I will not bore you with place names and things, suffice it

to say that, after a sharp opening, hounds divided. George scrubbed after one lot, and I huffed and puffed after the others. When my horse was down to an unhappy walk, I managed to get hold of my lot, and as we were near the boxes, we put them in, and people firmly took my horse away from me. By a happy chance there was a disused motor bike hard by, and it was suggested to the proprietor that he did not mind if the Master borrowed it, did he?

To be honest, the bike was not quite up to my weight, as well as being a bit green. It put me down three times going across the hill. Each time there was an anguished wail from the distant proprietor who had leaped into a Land-Rover to try and keep tabs on his property. However, we eventually found George who had run right off the hill, on the other side, and was grinding to a halt.

On the flat map, my lot ran twenty-three miles and George's twenty-five. The nice lad got his bike back, by the way, and I am quite certain that those bits were already bent before I got on it.

The next bit contains lust, politics and a labrador: so it should have something to interest anyone who reads this august magazine.

Once upon a time there was a young man who was desperately fond of hunting. His one desire was to hunt a pack of foxhounds. Fiscal realities being what they were, this desire seemed to be an unrealistic one, a fact that his father pointed out to him in well-measured terms. So the lad was sent as an indentured serf to the great chartered accountancy mines in the City of London.

No Big Bang for him; chained to a Dickensian stool, he spent his days 'casting', which has nothing to do with fishing and everything to do with adding up endless columns of pounds, shillings and pence. This was done manually; the chief reckoned that the desire to use an adding machine indicated a lack of moral fibre.

There was another foul ploy called 'Blotting and Ticking', which involved two serfs, one with the cash book and the other with a ledger, monotonously calling the entries to each other, ticking and blotting as they went. Biographical pens were frowned on; the inkwell and the Waverly pen nib were still to the fore ('They came as a boon and a blessing to men, the Pickwick, the Owl, and the Waverly pen'.)

Our particular serf spent most of his time dreaming of wet green fields, across which he and his hounds were squandering, as a result of which his casting, and his blotting and ticking, was deemed to be of less than the high standard demanded by his masters. Nor was the lad's social life a mitigation. He tended to spend his spare time reading Surtees and practising his hunting horn in the wardrobe where his standard accountancy suit hung.

These somewhat deviant practices found little favour with the other inhabitants of the flat, who felt that the youth should be spending his time on more productive study, like women, or something.

As part of the 'or something' category, it was decreed that our rustic lad should accompany the other flat-dwellers to attend upon the monthly revels of the Kensington Young Conservatives, where the dough of correct political thought was theoretically leavened by the chance of a bit of nooky. Indeed it turned out that for once practice accorded with political theory, because our hero discovered a plump but pleasant girl, who not only appeared fascinated by his thoughts on the influence of South Dorset Salesman '44 in the establishment of the modern foxhound, but even consented to allow him to take her home.

It being a balmy night in high summer, what could have been more natural than for the young couple to make a detour into Kensington Gardens? There they sought a bit of comfort in some convenient boscage, either to see if it might hold a fox, or to discuss the famous dictum of the then Prime Minister that they 'had never had it so good'.

Whatever, it really became a most engrossing discussion, until the youth felt something cold and wet intruding where cold, wet things should not have been, at that particular time. It quickly became obvious that the cold, wet thing was a nose. The nose was attached to a large black labrador which, even at that stressful moment, our hero realized must be a 'sniffer' dog only doing its bit.

Attached to the labrador were two very large policemen, who were 'Ho-Ho-ing', and 'what have we got here, Bert, thenning', as only highly-trained products of Hendon Training School can. Explanations of political discussions were received with rather gratuitous ribaldry, and it was pointed out that whatever it was that our Young Conservatives were doing, to do it in a Royal Park, 'within sight and sound of Their Royal Highnesses, I shouldn't wonder', was at best a Breach of the Peace, and might well be construed as High Treason, they shouldn't wonder. Particulars were taken down, and pulled up, and the unhappy couple were dismissed into physical and spiritual outer darkness.

Such an unfortunate happening was bound to put a strain on a burgeoning relationship, however promising. History does not relate what happened to the maiden in the case.

However, it is known that the young man reverted to reading Surtees, practising his hunting horn and failing his accountancy exams. He was subsequently expelled from the City, and became a Master of Foxhounds. As such he continues to this day, a saddened and embittered figure, with an abiding, and totally unreasonable, dislike of Young Conservatives and black labradors.

February always used to be one of my favourite hunting months. In recent years the weather has spoiled things after Christmas, but I must say that since the snow went we have been having some real old-fashioned sport. The weather has been settled, the foxes are lying out in the sunshine and the dog foxes are travelling.

We had a good hunt last week from a bit of country which has not been over-flush with foxes these last years. Anyway we found this fox and thundered away, and it soon became apparent that he was a traveller, with his head set for the back hills. We started off on some lovely sound white grass, and all our visitors galloped with a gay abandon. Then hounds began to climb, and it got rougher and wetter and steeper. I watched one party of low-country people set off with one of our hill artists as their guide. I thought to myself that they would do well to stay with him, for he skims the hills like a swallow; they did not, and for all I know they are up there yet. I just hope that someone finds them before they finish eating their horses and start on each other.

So what of James in all this wild haroosh? You do not hunt hounds for as long as I have without developing a little cunning, so I took a neat little inside turn that would put me ahead of the game. Hounds promptly turned out and left me the wrong side of a nasty steep valley; it is this knack I have, you see, blast it. We were getting up into some queer country, at this stage, but I was getting upsides of the first flight, when the old horse disappeared into a bog; it is this knack I have, you see. The country we were in now is better if you ride ten stone than eighteen, so my progress did not get any faster. I knew that if hounds continued their headlong career in the direction they appeared to be going, then a helicopter would be my only hope.

In a five-mile radius of where we were only about two tractors existed. One of them just happened to be browsing, or whatever tractors do up there, in the path of the fox, which promptly got the hump and turned off at an angle; for which relief, much thanks. Another long, wet climb had the old horse down to a walk, and my fettle was not improved by the Vice-Chairman squirting past me. Do you know what the bounder had done? He had only dragged his unfortunate wife from her horse, pinched her flask, and galloped off leaving her, naked and howling (emotionally, not physically), with his heaving animal and empty flask. I found his fleeting remarks about second horses in very poor taste. Only five horses got the end of the hunt. I was fifth out of five, and they had eaten the fox

by the time I got there. Anyway I had a nip out of Mrs Vice-Chairman's flask, although there was not much left in that either, and the old horse had a breather, which he richly deserved after some seventeen miles, with a 7-mile point.

We have a problem that I suspect prevails in many hunting countries, which is that one end of the country always feels that it gets less hunting than the other. In particular, people complain that we spend too much time in the 'valley'. This has to be put in perspective. The valley is ten miles long, and cuts through the middle of the hills; it is very difficult to meet within five miles of it without running into the valley. However, as the valley is surrounded by our best country, I have to admit that I do not make strenuous efforts to avoid going there, and if you knew it, neither would you.

By the time you read this, many people will have finished their season. The pressures of modern farming are such that many hunts have to stop hunting early in March. Very few feel able to continue into April, and only a small number look to catch a May fox. The Lakeland packs do lambing calls right through into May, but that has always been the tradition there. My feelings about spring hunting are ambivalent. I enjoy hunting with someone else in April, but I am happy to shut up my own shop at the end of March. We start in August, and by the end of March, hunting has become stale. I suppose that my stamina is not what it used to be, but it is not entirely that.

When I first started hunting hounds, we used to go on right through April, and I did not enjoy it even then: there are too many ifs and buts about spring hunting to make it fun for the management. I think that nature makes it plain when it is time to stop, because the foxes disappear. There is not much pleasure for the huntsman, or his hounds, in spending hours in fruitless drawing. The ladies and gentlemen may consider it a 'lovely day for riding about', but that is not the point of foxhunting so far as I am concerned. There is not much mystery about where the foxes are, as your hounds will tell you, as they mark hole after hole, and they do not understand why they keep being taken away. I have no desire to disturb the vixens, and will do so only at the request of a farmer or shepherd – after all, their lamb crop is their livelihood. If one does find a fox and have a hunt in April, the fox's one desire is to quit the hills and get down in bye, where the lambing is in full swing. Lambing is a time of great stress. When you are working twenty hours a day, and coping with all the myriad problems that occur at that time, the last thing you want is a pack of hounds through your lambing park, however fond of hunting you may be; I know very well that I would not want it.

There should not be any lambs on the hills before the middle of April, but accidents will happen, and some hill tups seem to be able to squeeze through keyholes to get the jump (if you will pardon the expression) on their fellows. The prospect of mother and child being separated is another worry. It all adds up to half-cock hunting, to which I am temperamentally unsuited. But it is fun to go and have a day with somebody else, and let them take the strain. Even if it is a bad day's hunting, it is very often a lovely day for riding about.

Wise men know that the safest place to have a breeding vixen is in the middle of their lambing field. Not only will she not touch a lamb, but she will also discourage outsiders from messing on her territory. Once I farmed a piece of land that was not only surrounded by forestry on three sides, but also had a breeding earth in the middle of it, where there was a litter every year. The only time I had a problem was one year with a sickly twin. When I did my morning round, the lamb was lying alone, up a hedge back; it was alive, but covered in tiny toothmarks. I can only conclude that the cubs had found it and thought that it was a grand thing to play with. I also conclude that mother must have given them all a good clip round the ear when she got home because it never happened again.

Near where my father lived there was an old-fashioned gamekeeper, of the keeper naturalist school. He called me in when I was passing one day, to 'have a look at this'. His hen run was at the bottom of his garden, with the hutch up against the field hedge. A vixen reared five cubs under the hutch. The cubs used to play out in the field within sight of the totally unconcerned hens. The old man said that he'd never have any trouble as long as they bred there.

The fox is a fascinating animal. It always gives me a thrill to see one. They are such wonderful movers; I wish my hounds could all move as well! To hunt and catch the fox is the great joy of my life, but I have never yet harmed a fox except on a hunting day, and I hope that I shall never be in a position where I feel that I have to. I am looking forward to the day when there is a breed in my present lambing field; they will be most welcome.

I saw a most interesting Lionel Edwards print the other day, one which I have never seen before. It shows a hunt collected in a village street. The hounds are being held up, stage left. Centre stage is a dismounted hunt servant who is washing a dead fox in a bucket of water, a course of action that rather intrigued me. I mean one does not get a lot of that sort of thing these days.

As luck would have it, on the back of the picture there was a bit of paper that explained what was going on. This was the Old Berks at a place called Harwell, in 1908. The fox had apparently been killed in a sewage drain, and was being washed before the last rites.

I found this quite fascinating, but begging more questions than it answered. For instance were the Old Berks hounds so fastidious that they had to have their foxes washed for them before they would deign to eat them? To judge from the picture they were not much worried one way or the other. Half of them are not even looking at the fox, some appear to be scratching. All in all it would seem that they lacked venom. I am quite certain that my hounds would have been across the road in one second flat, would have eaten the fox, sewage, bucket and all, and would probably have taken the hand off the prat who was waving it about.

However, no doubt things were more genteelly done in Berkshire in 1908. I wonder if the man with the bucket was not a whipper-in, but a washer-up; did he gallop about the country with a bucket clanking on his saddle Ds? Was there a case on his saddle containing sponge, towel and Stephanotis Bath Essence? Even perhaps a rubber duck? I suspect that there was more to this than met the eye.

On the right of the picture there is a large moustachioed gent who is quite plainly the Gaffer. Centre left is a comely lady riding side saddle. It is my opinion that the Comely Lady wants a brush, and the Master wants . . . well, to give her the brush, and to earn a few brownie points which he can cash in at the first possible opportunity. No lady is going to respond very much to a sewage-flavoured trophy, so Bert comes clanking up with his bucket to give the fox a quick lick and a promise. How fortunate that nice Mr Edwards was there to capture the scene for the bewilderment of posterity.

By the time you read this I shall have put my hunting horn in the case for the last time. I view the prospect of no longer hunting hounds with mixed feelings; twenty-one years is a big slice of a lifetime, and of course I shall miss it. On the other hand, it will be nice to go hunting without being in a state of complete nervous prostration. It will be nice to sit on a hilltop occasionally and watch hounds on the other side without feeling that one really ought to negotiate that bloody awful crossing to go and interfere with them. It will be nice to pontificate on what the huntsman should be doing at any given moment, secure in the knowledge that I am no longer going to have to put my theories into practice. In fact, I am going to be a real old bore and a thorough nuisance to everybody, and that prospect I thoroughly relish.

At least I know that my successor will make a good job of it. I remember a certain eminent MFH who gave up hunting hounds and made a point of employing a totally useless huntsman, so that people would keep coming up and telling him how much better it was when he was hunting the hounds. The old man used to love it, and preen himself no end. It did not seem to worry him that his hounds were being ruined; it would certainly worry me.

There is undoubtedly one big difference between hunting now and hunting in the early sixties; it is much more popular now. Twenty-five years ago there seemed to be very few young people hunting and not much general enthusiasm; in fact, hunting seemed to be going gently into a coma. How things have changed. Most packs now seem to be at bursting point and, perhaps best of all, there is a new generation of hunting farmers. When I was young the older farmers hunted, or had hunted, but the sons did not, by and large. Now their sons and daughters have come back to it in a big way and that must be good for the future of hunting.

Another big change has been the evolvement of shooting from a sport to a business. I suppose that with rising costs and other pressures, it is an inevitable progression, but I think it is a pity if shooting people totally lose sight of their sporting roots. I think that shooting should be more than just an asset on a balance sheet from which the maximum dividend must be extracted.

I was watching the lissom form of our lady whipper-in skimming across the hill the other day. And amongst the other idle thoughts that were jostling their way through my brain, was the question as to whether there should not be a female form of whipper-in. After all, whipper-in is not a very feminine appellation and, I suppose, just might conjure up visions of Ms Cynthia Payne's parties. We certainly do not want those sort of visions creeping into a family magazine: they might cause some old 12-bore to go off half cock, I should not wonder. So on all counts I suggest that something more genteel is called for.

I considered *whippette*, but discarded it after chewing it for a while. It might just upset the coursing people, and on no account would I wish to do such a thing. A whippette also sounds too like a cheer person for an American football team, and conjures up visions of long, slim thighs, very short skirts, twirling pom poms, and . . . steady, James, steady; remember the blood pressure. Although, come to think of it, why not Hunt cheer leaders? It would brighten up all those dreary meets when one spends hours while the Hon Sec is in the pub 'taking the cap'. I just might moot the idea at the next Supporters' Club meeting.

But we stray from the point. It finally seemed that there was only one answer; whipperene. It is professionalism combined with femininity and grace. What more could anyone ask?

I am just recovering from a debilitating dose of influenza, which you may regard as being hardly the stuff that headlines are made of. The only thing of interest about it is that when I lived in the south and west I suffered horribly from colds and sinus and such like illnesses, including an average of two nasty goes of 'flu every winter. Since I have lived in the Borders, I have never had a cold, only occasional bouts of sinusitis, and 'flu only twice in five years. So what do we make of that? That the Border air suits my constitution, I suppose; it is certainly strong stuff.

There is another factor to be taken into account. About

seven years ago I read somewhere that red wine was good for the health, something to do with fagocytes, or something. Since then I have taken a glass of wine every winter's night and have seldom seen fit to discontinue the practice during the summer. I do not know if it has done me any good, but I think that it has done me good, which amounts to the same thing. In case this makes you click your teeth, let me refer you to First Timothy 5.23: '. . . use a little wine for thy stomach's sake and thine often infirmities.' I do not find St Paul a very sympathetic character, on the whole, but on this issue we are one.

A kind letter from a gentleman in California, USA. It seems that James has permeated into the Californian consciousness, and as I am degradeable, non-pollutant, and environment compatible, there seems every possibility that were I to be run up the flagpole in Silicone Valley, all the Yuppies would salute me. This is obviously going to be the answer for me now that I have ceased to hunt hounds; I shall go to California and become a cult.

I have some dark glasses somewhere, and I do not need a chest wig, but I shall have to get one of those medallion things for when I have my shirt open to the waist. I shall have to practise that a bit. But I fancy that it would only be a matter of a short time before I had lots of white suits and a white Roller. Then I would come back and be interviewed by that portly Irish chap on the telly, and you could all say, 'Coo look, there's James; he's a Cult, he is. Didn't I always say so, Mother? A proper Cult.'

I was looking through my old diaries and I came across the 'Case of the Phantom Horn-Blower'. I was drawing a field of kale this day when there came wafting on the breeze what I thought to be the sound of a hunting horn being blown without a great deal of expertise. This was at a time when the antis had been very busy with a nearby pack, and all our lads had had their boots retacketed, and were going about cracking their knuckles, and saying things like, 'Thirky old boys better hadn't come by yere, you,' which should enable you to place the area fairly accurately, I should think.

Anyway there I was, drawing, and the horns of Elfland softly blowing. I mildly suggested to the terrierman that he should investigate, and immediately there were Land-Rovers driving furiously to all points of the compass, filled to bursting point by large men with cudgels. I wondered what I had unleashed.

They returned somewhat crestfallen. They had indeed discovered the Phantom. He lived in a council house and played the trombone. It is difficult to reconcile the two, and the poor lad was banished to sit on a water trough in the middle of a 100-acre field. I thought it did not quite sound like a hunting horn; it did not sound much like the 'St Louis Blues' either, but that is a personal opinion.

INDEX

Aberdeen, climate 125
accountancy 230–1
addresses 80
Admiralty 152
advertising, and hunting 46
advice, from quotations 28–9
aeroplanes, to Dublin 205–6
agricultural shows 35–6, 186
Al Maktoum, Sheikh Hamdan 70
Americanisms 71–2, 73, 167
anonymous letters 73
Army 90–1, 149, 189–90
arthritis 120
artificial insemination 175–6
ATV *see* vehicles, All-Terrain
Australia 153

BAALAM society 102
bagpipes 85–6
Baily's Hunting Directory 68, 69
bales, stacking 150–1
banks, jumping 11
barbed wire 47–8
beaglers, pudgy 214
Beaufort, 9th Duke of 58
bed-making 87
Birmingham, sewage 184–5
Black Lane, Dartmoor 113
bleepers, for terriers 224–5
bogs, on Dartmoor 112–13
Boxing Day, hunting on 81, 83, 163–4
bracken 62
British Motor Industry 89

California 241
calls of nature 99
caravans 74, 123
cattle 57–8
champagne 215–16
children, of huntsmen 98
Christmas cake 209
Christmas Eve, hunting on 81–2
Cirencester, Royal Agricultural College 199–200
civil servants 141–2
clergy, capacity for venom 103
climate, effect of 125–6
clothes 19–22, 55–6, 130, 193; outdoor 220–2
coat-hangers, for dowsing 138–9
colds 99–100
collective nouns 215
Combined Cadet Force 190
commons 173–4
Cornwall 56–7, 125, 167; hunting in wind 166
Country Landowners' Assoc. 97–8
cricket 64–5
cubhunting 15, 17–18, 40–2, 62–3; *see also* hunting
cults 241
curses 110

damp, in stables 120
Dartmoor 112–13, 132
deafness 141
declining hunting 126–7
dentists, Australian 153

Devon and Somerset, song 124
dialect 59–60; Northumbrian 140–1
direction, sense of 192–3
dogs 84, 181; bearded collies 160–2; bleepers for 224–5; collie 108–9; driving 155–6; the Fraggle 117–18; 181; illnesses 208; Kelpie 191; Labrador 232; Patterdale (Jessica Jane) 117–18, 181, 191–2, 204; terriers 92, 106, 224–5; *see also* hounds
domestic servants 145, 184
doubt, regional differences 182–3
dowsing 138–9
drains 177–8; *see also* sewage
driving, carriage 121–3; drunken 155–6; *see also* roads
Drought, Minister of 143
drove roads 90
drugs, in greyhound racing 100–1
Dublin 199, 206; Show 187, 207
dukes 6, 172–3

ear-tags, misuse of 148
Edwards, Lionel, print by 237
eels 220
Exmoor 229

Fiery Jack, cure for gout 80
fishing 190–1
flooding, West Country 164
Fox, Charles James 85
foxes 41–2, 72; in films 44–5; and game birds 156; and hens 237; and lambing 236–7; names for 85; shooting 18–19; washing 237–8; *see also* hunting, cubhunting
Free Boy Scheme 178
free trips 200–1
friends, meeting 51–3

game birds 156, 162–3
Game Fair 54–5, 200–1
gamefowl 228–9
gates 97–8
geese, Brent 91
gentry, official demise of 185
German character 125
Germany, stacking bales 150–1
girl grooms 215
goats 65–6
gondolas 204
Goodson, Sir Alfred 171
gossip 52–3, 189
gout 80
greyhound racing 100–1
Grimling 130, 145, 184, 205
grouse 69–70
Gulbenkian, Nubar 123

hacking home 60–1
Hamburg 90
hats, bowler 172; flat 133; top 19–20
hay 169
health 212–14, 240–1
hill shepherds, leanness of 213
hills 113, 212–14; hunting on 138, 212
HOJLAC society 134
holidays 50–1, 123–4, 186
Honiton Hound Show 229
Honourable Artillery Company 149
horse dealers 134
horse shows 34
horse-drawn vehicles 122
horses, brakeless 154; cob 62, 64, 138; dummy 104; from Hamburg 90; hermaphrodite 65;

for jumping 11; mileage of 107; for moors 12
hound shows 36–7, 66, 186, 207
hounds 6, 94; and barbed wire 47–8; control of 135–6; exercising 136–7; feeding 61–2; homing instinct 84; illnesses 208; mileage 108, 154; naming of 71; painted 67; recognition of 179; steadiness to wallabies and wolves 46–7; ugly 84–5; Welsh 71; young 15, 18, 62–3
houses, cold 160; new 197, 210
hovercraft 194
howitzers, bale 150–1
hubris 139, 208
Hudson, W. H. 90
hunt ball 218–19
Hunt Chairmen 96, 196, 215
Hunt Secretaries 215
hunt servants 74–6, 95
hunt supporters 139–40
hunting 3–5, 7, 72, 92–4, 96–7, 102, 233–5; advice 28–9; at Christmas 81–2, 83; in autumn 15–18, 201–2; fashionable 92; on hills 138, 212; in hot weather 216; on motor bike 229–30; neighbouring packs 109–10; nerve 27; newspaper reports 170–1; Opening Meet 42–4; popularity of 239; rough country 211–12; in snow 5–6; in Spain 51; in spring 235; in wind 165–6, 176–7; *see also* cubhunting
hunting caps 20–1
hunting flasks 10
hunting horn 223–4, 226, 241
hunting songs 124–5
hygiene, patron saints of 143–5

Imber 91
imposters 120
influenza 240
Ireland 204; *see also* Dublin, Louth, Ulster

James, Mrs 8, 39, 74, 82, 95–6, 142; and deafness 141; and the Fraggle 117, 118, 181; and holidays 50–1, 186, 193–6; and lies 159; moving house 197; and royal wedding 201; sense of direction 192–3; and tanker deliveries 170; and telephones 49, 192
James, Mrs, the elder 163–4, 216–17, 222–3
Jermyn Street 55–6, 133, 165
jumping fences 11–13

keepers, and foxes 22–3
kennels 61–2
kenning 178–9
Kiribati 53

labour exchanges 105
lady masters 95–6, 102–3, 134, 196, 215
Lake District hunting, season 235; songs 124
lambing *see* sheep
Land Agents 118–20
Larkhill 91
Latin phrases 132–3
Lent Sheep 131–2
lies 158–9
London 99, 188, 210–11; annual shirt trip 55–6, 133, 193
Louth, Co, drunken driving 155–6
luncheon, fashionable hunts 92

macaws, as game birds 162–3
machinery 197–8
Masters of Foxhounds 1–3, 8, 30–1, 114, 215; challenge cup for 25–7; character of 1–3, 53, 139–40; ex- 23, 24–5, 165; home-bred *v.* imported 127–9; new 114–15, 164–5, 196; physical standards for 226–8; training of 31–3; types 76–9
Masters of Foxhounds Association 226–8
Maynard, Joan 174–5
Mazawattee Tea recipe 10
medical students 147
millstones, sailing 145
mink 100, 183
motor bicycles 41, 229–30
musical evenings 124, 130–1

National Foxhunting College 31–3
National Parks 174–5
New Year 83–4
New Zealand Green-Lipped Mussel pills 120
Newcastle, Eldon Square Shopping Centre 192
newspapers, 170–1, 205
newts, drunken 151–2
Northumberland, dialect 140–1; pipes 86

old men 58–9, 86–7
Opening Meet 42–4
otter hunting 183
Outdoor Man 221–2

Paris 186, 194
peat hags 146
Pennsylvania, USA, geese in 91
Percy Special recipe 10
Peterborough Show 37
pig swill 105–6
place names 37–9
Pony Club camp 81
pot ale syrup 169
pots, chamber, rubber 22
public lavatories 175
puppy shows 34, 134
Putney Vale 87

quotations 28–9, 179

racehorses 142
racial prejudice 118
railways 68–9, 133; Spanish 195–6; steam engines 167–8
Ramblers' Association 112
rape in hunting field 48
retirement 238–9
Rizzo, John 153
roads 94–5, 142, 143
Royal Agricultural College, Circencester 199–200
Royal Calpe hounds 51
royal wedding 201
Rydal Show 39

St Paul 241
saints, Cornish 145; patron 143–4
SAMBO society 23, 24–5
scent, before snow 7, 117; in bracken 62; unpredictability of 6, 70, 97
school concert 148
science, application of 224–6
scientific research 180
Scotland, landowners in 70
second horses 92, 234
sewage, Birmingham 184–5
sheep, dipping 131–2, 201;

droving 229; Ewe Scheme 209–10; lambing 111, 181, 185–6, 236; recognition of 178–9; tourists and 14
shooting 40, 42, 162–3, 202–3
show widowers 34–5
shows 33–7
signals 203
Skibereen, climate 125–6
snow 5–6, 7–8, 164
social conscience 121
social workers, Australian 153
socio-economic groups 185
Spain 51, 130, 216–17; travel to 193–6
speakers, at Shepherds' Suppers 88, 158
stag parties, 146–8
stallions, cart 168
suppers, Shepherds' and Farmworkers' 87–8, 157–8
Swedish Navy 152

tankers, delivery 169–70
teeth, false 222–4
telephones 8–9, 49, 192
television 44–6, 224, 225–6
terrier shows 35
terriers 92, 106, 224–5
Territorial Army 149
Thirsk 68–9
Tories 47
tornado of mist 157
tourists, drawbacks of 13–15
towns, twinning of 67–8
training, of hunt servants 75; of MsFH 31–3
trains *see* railways
travel, foreign 124, 199–200
tricycle *see* vehicles, All-Terrain
Turin, cable television 225–6
turkeys 82–3

Ulster, addresses in 80
United States 20–1, 67, 91, 241
university 198
Urban Man 211

vehicles 88–9; All-Terrain 106, 107, 137, 225; horse-drawn 122; in London 210–11
Vice-Chairman 73, 234
video films 81, 226
village life 188–9
Virginia, USA, hunting garb 20–1
visiting cards 183–4
visitors 210
visitors' book 131

Wales 61
wallabies 46
water, jumping 13
Western Horseman 104
whippers-in, lady 239–40; *see also* hunt servants
whips 137
whisky, over-indulgence 220
Willoughby de Broke, Lord 33
Wiltshire Downs 90–1
wind 160, 165–6, 177
wine, for health 241
wives, usefulness of 74, 210
wolves 46–7

Youth Training Scheme 178